WOVOKA, THE INDIAN MESSIAH

GREAT WEST AND INDIAN SERIES X

BOOKS BY PAUL BAILEY

Fiction

TYPE HIGH

FOR THIS MY GLORY

THE GAY SAINT

SONG EVERLASTING

Mystery Fiction

DELIVER ME FROM EVA

Biography

SAM BRANNAN AND THE CALIFORNIA MORMONS

JACOB HAMBLIN, BUCKSKIN APOSTLE

FABULOUS FARMER
THE STORY OF WALTER KNOTT AND HIS BERRY FARM
(with Roger Holmes)

WALKARA, HAWK OF THE MOUNTAINS

WOVOKA, THE INDIAN MESSIAH

Editor and Compiler of

THE MORMONS IN CALIFORNIA
PIONEER JOURNAL OF WILLIAM GLOVER

WOVOKA
The Indian Messiah

by PAUL BAILEY

WESTERNLORE PRESS . . . LOS ANGELES 41

ANDERSEN

To Edward A. Dyer
who knew Wovoka

TABLE OF CONTENTS

TABLE OF ILLUSTRATIONS

ACKNOWLEDGMENTS

IN HIS monumental and definitive study of the messianic movements which have swept the various tribes of American Indians from the Delaware Prophet down to his inclusive and sympathetic examination of Wovoka and his doctrine and ghost dance, James Mooney did his world of readers, and the white man in general, a great service. Without that impressive volume, published under sponsorship of the Bureau of American Ethnology, little that was truth would ever have been known about the Paiute Messiah and the strange and far-reaching religion he brought forth. No author can ever go very far in interpreting the Wovokan riddle without leaning heavily on Mooney, his on-the-spot field studies of the ghost dance, and the great book which emerged from it.

Out of the Nevada Galilee where the Messiah spent his entire ministry came help to the author from sources close to the man himself. Alice Wilson Vidovich, daughter of Jack Wilson (Wovoka), of Schurz, Nevada, was most kind to me, even in face of the unkind things many writers have said about her father. To Edward A. Dyer, octogenarian of Fallon, Nevada, who not only knew Wovoka intimately but was Mooney's actual interpreter during his visit and interview with the Paiute Messiah, the author owes a great debt. In equal measure this debt extends to his son, Edward Dyer, Jr., who made available his own preservation of his father's words and pioneer experiences as they were dictated and written down.

In Yerington, Nevada, within a few miles of the site where the ghost dance had its inception, and where memory or knowledge of the Messiah is still fresh in the minds of many of the town's residents, came help from Charles A. McLeod, Mrs. Beth Wilson Ellis, Mrs. Velma Ford James, members of the city recorder's office, and many others.

To M. W. Stirling, director Smithsonian Institution, Bureau of American Ethnology, for opening the Bureau's photographic files to the enhancement of this book, and to J. E. Reynolds of Van Nuys, California, for use that was made of his pictorial Indian collection, I tender my sincere thanks.

And finally, to Colonel Tim McCoy, of Hollywood, California, whose lifelong interest in the Wovokan legend, research on the subject, and personal visit to

Acknowledgments

the Messiah—all rich material made available to the author—a great debt is acknowledged.

To all these interested parties, kind friends, and those of necessity left unmentioned, the author stands humbly and deeply grateful. No man builds a book entirely alone.

WOVOKA, THE INDIAN MESSIAH

I

SON OF A PROPHET

The Pilgrim Fathers landed on the shores of America and fell upon their knees. Then they fell upon the aborigines. —AUTHOR UNKNOWN.

A MERICA'S dealings with its Indian population stands as an indictment. The record of its drivings, its bloody extermination, its land theft, and its treaty repudiation, is no happy thing to examine. This blot upon our honor as a nation seems never to fade with time. And it is almost incredible that the final crowning infamy of the white man against his red brother—the massacre which broke the back and heart of the American Indian, wiped away the final vestige of his collective dignity, and sent the last of the great chiefs, Sitting Bull, to the grave—came about through the blundering misunderstanding of a nationwide religious revival whose basic tenets were closely akin to those of Jesus of Nazareth.

The voice of its revelation was Wovoka, the humble prophet who, at the turn of the century, claimed to have talked with God. And this prophet arose out of the mildest and least warlike of all tribes—the Nevada Paiute. In his little Nevada Galilee Wovoka taught a doctrine of peaceful acceptance of the white man's way. "You must not fight," he told his listeners. "Do no harm to anyone. Do right always." The new dance, allegedly taught him during one of his visits to heaven, was passed on to his brethren and carried back by his awed and reverent visitors to their own peoples. Tribes from coast to coast soon were dancing their own version of it, and the doctrine of Wovoka became topic of a thousand council fires.

The American military, mistakenly viewing it as another war dance, made every move to suppress it. But the revival was on, the words of Wovoka the Messiah gave new hope to the discouraged red man, and the "ghost dance" increased with frenzy in spite of the ban. Troops were dispatched to the trouble-spot. Hotchkiss guns were wheeled out and pointed in the red-man's direction. Then, as usual, the guns belched death. Indian bodies were piled up like cordwood. Sitting Bull and his elders were murdered. Once more the Great White Spirit had spoken.

* * * *

From the white man's viewpoint, Wovoka would scarcely rate as an impressive prophet, much less an heaven-visiting Messiah, simply because he did not look like one. Instead of robes, he dressed in white men's clothes. And even today, in his Nevada homeland, he is remembered only as Jack Wilson—the name white men gave him, and the name by which he answered to them. But, in spite of his Americanized name and dress, he was a full-blooded Paiute, heavily-framed and nearly six feet in height. He was born around 1858,[1] on the Walker River in Mason Valley, Nevada, and, except for a few short journeyings, lived out his entire lifetime in the valley of his birth. His spiritual leanings had something of background and authority, for Wovoka was the son of Tävibo, another Walker River Paiute prophet. It was Tävibo who gave his son the name of Wovoka, meaning "The Cutter," and it was Tävibo who doubtless passed on to this same son much of the mysticism and contemplative attributes which became the messianic complex of his later years. "The prophetic claims and teachings of the father, the reverence with which he was regarded by the people, and the mysterious ceremonies which were doubtless of frequent performance in the little tulé wikiup at home must have made early and deep impression on the mind of the boy, who seems to have been by nature of a solitary and contemplative disposition, one of those born to see visions and hear still voices."[2]

Tävibo died in 1870, leaving the 14-year-old Wovoka to fend for himself. And, from the family of David Wilson, who took the young and husky Indian boy on as a farm hand, came both the anglicized name and his white man leanings.[3] The Wilson brothers, David, William and George, had come into Nevada in 1863, seven years previous to Tävibo's death. While on their way into California, they had crossed into Mason Valley, noted the clear and swift-running Walker River, the tall and snow-capped mountains protectively surrounding it, the timbered foothills, and the rich and level bottomlands, and had concluded to go no farther. Without ceremony or permission they settled their families on the Paiute lands toward Pine Grove, the ancestral home of Tävibo, Wovoka, and their people. These Indians, of whom Wovoka was one, and their tulé wikiups, happening to be on the lands the Wilsons had pre-empted, simply became a part of their holdings. Within a few years the Wilsons returned to Missouri, gathered up a sizable herd of cattle, and drove them to their new homesteads in Nevada.

By that time other settlers had moved into the area, and the native Paiutes were being squeezed out of their homelands to the river margins or to the hills. They became the menials, to work the farms, and to do the chores of the white man. They like ten thousand other

Indians were at grips with relentless avarice. Like others, they soon were stripped of dignity and expelled from their land. The "settling-up" of Mason Valley happened quickly. Except for a few earlier skirmishes with the white man, the Paiutes had been comparatively peaceful and unwarlike. By the time the settlers had put up their barns and houses, it was too late. The dispossessed natives were given the privilege of joining their ousted brethren on the Pyramid Lake reservation, or remaining as working serfs to the whites. Wovoka elected, like others, to stay in his homeland. Stoically, he accepted his lot, and for the little pay and food it brought, as Indian "hand" to David Wilson.

The Wilsons gave small heed to the fact that he was an only son of the tribal *capita*. They cared nothing about his dreams or his thoughts. They taught him how to brand a calf, how to pitch hay, how to clean a stable, and how to handle a plow. They took him out of his rabbit-skins, and put him into white man's jeans. They cropped his hair to shortness, and commanded him in the white man's language, which he quickly learned. They taught him to sit on a chair when in their house, and not to squat on his hams on the floor. They gave him a white man's name—"Jack." And, since he now was white man in everything but color, and since he was Wilson's in everything but soul, he accepted the captivity by accepting the name. From that time forward he answered to "Jack Wilson."

The son of Tävibo envied the white man, and acknowledged the white man's superiority over the docile Paiutes. Deeply he was jealous of the Wilson children, and the advantages and consideration their white skins gave them. He studied them, and he aped them, unaware of how superficial was their actual hold upon him—for he was Indian, real and to the marrow. Daytimes, he stoically moved through the white man's circles. Nights he slept on the ground in his own tulé wikiup. Days he listened to white-man talk about their great possessions and their own great God. Nights he turned his eyes south to the towering Holy Mountain [Mount Grant], where the Paiute Great Father had given his people fire, and had taught them the arts of living before soaring off to the upper places of the Sunland. When he said his own Paiute prayer to dawn's first sun, he was talking with the tongue of Tävibo— and not in the manner of the white man.

II

In the Beginning

The deep cause of our world agony is that we have lost the passion and reverence for human personality and for the web of life and the earth which the American Indians have tended as a central, sacred fire since before the Stone Age. —JOHN COLLIER.

WOVOKA'S problem in adaptation to the white man's circle of living and thinking was made easier by the presence of William Wilson, or "Bill" as he generally was known, the Wilsons' oldest son of approximately Wovoka's age and, to a lesser degree by the two younger Wilson brothers, Joseph and George. A close bond of comradeship, which cut across all color and ethnic lines, quickly flowered between William Wilson and the lonely and imaginative Paiute orphan who had cast his lot with the Mason Valley rancher. Bill and Jack, as they came to be known, were inseparable. Wovoka slipped unresistingly into the role of Jack Wilson.

Bill taught Jack, the Indian, a workable English. Jack taught Bill, the American, a smattering of Paiute.

Their conversations were often a curious mixture of both. Jack took Bill and his brothers across Pine Grove to the sage-covered flatlands, where rabbits abounded. Bill saw to it that Jack became the possessor of a castoff but workable rifle that had once been his uncle's. Jack took his white brother down to the tulé huts of his tribesmen along the river, and made him known to the sullen occupants who brooded over their lost lands and dreamed on the revenge that someday they would unleash upon those who had stolen it from them.

Because the Son of Tävibo willed it, Bill Wilson was allowed to participate with the tribesmen in a rabbit hunt, Paiute style. The late fall frost lay heavy on the sage, when upwards of a hundred braves, with as many chattering squaws and children, gathered for the big drive. An entire hillside was enclosed with an immensely long net, staked upright, which the women had loosely woven from rush fibers. Men and boys, Bill and Jack included, armed with stout clubs, took their stance within the net. At a signal, the hillside became a laughing, howling bedlam as the Paiutes beat the earth and sage with clubs, driving the game from their burrows toward the great encircling net. Here the jackrabbits and cottontails became ensnared, or milled and circled in hopeless confusion, and here they were finished off by the relentless clubs of the squaws and youngsters. Afterwards the great heaps of rabbits were skinned and dressed for food, and their hides stretched to sapling frames for future blanket and clothing needs. All participants gorged themselves on fresh meat, roasted over glowing fires. And afterwards there was a dance of thanksgiving, in which Wovoka participated, while Bill Wilson looked on with envy.

But back at the ranch, in the face of its galling labors, and white man's ways, the Paiute lost all identity as a tribesman—to become plain Jack Wilson, an Indian hand in overalls. It has been said that a shovel was never made that would fit a Paiute, but the Wilson boys were hard workers, and Jack fell into toil's stride with them. The fact that this Paiute, at least, was a good worker, brought him ready favor with David Wilson, as rancher, so much so that no protest was made when Bill and the boys brought him into the house and allowed him to eat at their table, in preference to the trough-like handout area where other Paiutes received their food from the ranch owners.

The Wilson household was a new, and sometimes confusing world to the husky but shy Paiute, who looked and listened from its shadows. At the table he watched the family reverently bow their heads in prayer before partaking of food, then listened to the menfolk noisily thresh over the problems of the day as they ravenously consumed vast platters of food prepared by the tireless Mrs. Wilson and her daughters. In the evenings, before Wovoka retired to his own wikiup for the night, he would curiously watch as David Wilson took down the big sacred book and read of their God's dealings with His people.

From this book, and David Wilson's reading of it, he learned of how their Great Spirit made the world in six days, and then gave Himself a day in which to rest and feast. He learned of the place called the Garden of Eden, where there was plenty of wild game—deer, antelope, and rabbits—and where the first white man, Adam, and the first white woman, Eve, were happy because they had no worries, and their bellies were full of food. The white man's story of how their God fashioned and peopled the earth was a good one—but confusing in the light of how Tävibo had solemnly told him it *really* was done. In the wikiup, by the river, made alive by the smoke spirits and dancing light of their little fire, Tävibo had once made this mystery known to him.

"In the beginning, many many winters ago," Tävibo had said, "all the land between the big east mountains and the big west mountains was green with grass and rich with game. That was a long time before it got dry and full of sagebrush. In this pleasant land lived the

Lelangonappess, and as people, they were giants—taller than the pine trees that then grew in this land. The Lelangonappess were a happy race; they never quarreled or drew their bows in fight; their women were faithful, good, and comely to look upon.

"The great mountain fire was in the center of this land. There the sick and the injured were taken to breathe its magic vapors, which healed them in an instant. Into the fires of this mountain were cast the dead of the Lelangonappess, and the Great Spirit reclothed their frames with new flesh, and sped them joyfully to the happy hunting grounds.

"Surrounding this wonderful land were the high mountains of the snows, beyond which lived the Zhashmock—a fierce tribe of gaunt and hungry men. The Great Spirit forbade the Zhashmocks entering the green lands of the Lelangonappess, but occasionally they raided them in great force, and desperate were the battles that were fought to keep them out.

"After these wars the wounded and dead of the Lelangonappess were gathered up, and with songs and chants, were borne up the slopes of the mountain of fire. There the injured were healed, and the dead consumed by the flames. But one time during this great ceremony, a woman, heavy with child, was frightened by a bear. When her boy-child was born he was so crippled and misshapen that he became the object of ridicule from all the race of giants he had to live among. Strangely, the mountain's magic vapors failed to heal him, and the taunts and jeers of his people made him wish to die. Sadly the tormented and crippled youth climbed the mountain to cast himself into the flames. But suddenly, as he stood on the brink of the consuming fire, thunder shook the earth, and lightning split the heavens. In blinding light the Great Spirit stepped down from a cloud, and stood upon a mountain top. In wrath he cursed the Lelangonappess people for their cruelty to this boy. Deep into the bowels of the fire he spoke, and then he picked up the deformed young man, and three times dipped him into the flames. And from these flames the boy emerged—perfect, glorious and as bright as the Great Spirit himself.

"Amid great thunder the Great Spirit vanished, taking with him the boy. The beautiful land became brown and shriveled. The earth shook, the rocks split. The great giant of the lower world bellowed in his wrath. Two days this awful thing continued, until flame had split the magic mountain asunder, and melted rock flowed down into the once green valley.

"Wherever the Lelangonappess fled, the molten rock followed, until its heat had shrunk them down to the size of man, and burned their skins to dark brown. And then, amid this misery, the Zhashmocks attacked—and the Lelangonappess were massacred. Only one man and one woman survived, because they had hidden themselves in a cave. The man's name was Paiute. He and his woman were forced from that time forward to walk on the cooling surface of the rock that covered their once green land, and to live on a few rabbits and birds that had escaped the devastation.

"And that is how our people came to be," Tävibo had said. "And that is why our people never cease to be kind and generous toward the crippled ones who live among us."

From David Wilson, and Mrs. Wilson, as they read from the big book on evenings and the day of rest, he had learned much about the white man's Great Spirit, and *his* dealings. Wovoka knew that if he listened unobtrusively from the room's dark corners; kept his friendship with Mrs. Wilson and the boys, and showed smile and willingness to Mr. David, he would be a welcome Indian in the house. And, so long as he could stay in their house, he would let wonder and knowledge from the big book sink into his memory like water into the dry earth of summer. What he wanted to know about was the world of spirits, where men went to when they died. For, in this matter, he noted, the white man was just as concerned as was the Indian. And it would be good to know all that Tävibo knew about such things; and all that the white man and his big book knew of such things. Then would one, indeed, be wise.

Particularly was he entranced by the stories they read about Jesus—that great paleface medicine man, who lived so long ago, and did so much that was magic among his people. This Jesus could touch a man, and he would shake off his sickness. He could make plain water into firewater; he could take one small trout, and with a pass of the hand, turn it into enough fish to feed his whole tribe; he could breathe on a dead man, and the dead man's eyes would open once again into life.

This man Jesus, along with his magic, and his healings, taught his people many good things. He admonished them to love one another, and not to hate; that killings were all wrong; that peace was always better than war; that gentleness, kindness, patience, contemplation of the Great Spirit and his ways, and the desire to do good, constituted the one true way into the world of spirits when breath vanished from the body. Jesus claimed to be the son of God, but there had been unbelievers among his people. In spite of the wonders Jesus had taught them, the magic he had done among them, and that anyone could see he was the greatest of all medicine men and dreamers, they killed him by nailing him up to a board. But that only sped him straight to the spirit world. And after talking to his Great Father, he came back to life in three days. Breath came back into his body. He arose from the place they had put him, and walked once more among his people. And to prove that he was Jesus, he showed them the wounds in his hands.

Ah, but Jesus *was* a great medicine man, and a worker of wonders. To die three days, and then come alive, was a feat. To heal the sick, and to talk great truths, made him mighty among his believers. Wovoka was happy to learn these many things about Jesus. He seldom discussed the things he heard with the Wilson boys, but in the solitude of his little wikiup, he practiced the hand-magic Tävibo had taught him, and he stared himself into dreams about the spirit world and the life to come. He wished he were a white man, and could go to the white spirit world. And what would it be like to be a great prophet and worker of wonders, like Jesus? And what would it be like to die three days; visit the other world; talk to God; and return to life, and tell people of the things one had seen?

III

Blood Brothers

Since the Indians could not write, the history of their wars has been set down by their enemies, and the story has been told always from the hostile point of view. White writers have lauded white courage and claimed white successes. If it has been necessary to confess defeat, they have abused those who overcame them, as the defeated always abuses the victors. —GEORGE BIRD GRINNELL.

THE Wilson family, being one of the first to settle in Mason Valley, had made the most of their free choice of land. The bench-land toward the southern mountains which picturesquely ringed the valley, unlike the bottom areas tapering toward the river, was timbered in juniper and scrub pine. This stretch, which became known as Pine Grove, rich in shade patch and mountain grasses, was ideally suited to them for the running of cattle, and they had taken in enough of the sage-covered flatlands for their necessary crop-raisings of wheat and alfalfa. Pine Grove, however, being the ancestral hunting-grounds for deer, bear and piñon nuts, was just as essential and important to the Walker River Paiutes. The Wilsons were not the only white men who had grabbed off the rich and timbered areas. Fences were going up everywhere, as the settlers moved in, and one choice earth-spread after another was cut away from the Indian homelands. Paiute resentment over this catastrophic loss was widespread. The tribal elders, at the council fires, were bitterly vociferous of this rape of their homelands. Past victories were recounted; dances were held to shake off the apathy of this Paiute generation who, unresistingly, were allowing themselves to be robbed of their heritage and pressed into peonage to the whites.

But the Paiutes were not as the fierce plains Indians. Peaceful, docile, friendly, and inclined toward the lazy way of life, they had been easy prey. Chief Winnemucca was gone; their fighting days were over. In vain the tribal elders called for a revival of the warfare that once had stood them out as men, and had brought them glory on the field of battle. But the Paiutes were finished—individually and collectively. Winnemucca was dead, and none other like him had risen to lead on against the hopeless fight. They now had their choice—to be reservation Indians, or serve the white man in his plowings and plantings of their ancestral homeland.

Wovoka, recipient of the pressure from both factions, and confusedly growing into manhood, had unresistingly slipped into the latter role. As the son of Tävibo, he had heard much of the glories of Winnemucca and those days when the Paiute stood up for his rights. From the Wilsons he had learned how to sit in a chair, eat at a table, and dress the white man's way. Like other Paiute farm-hands in Mason Valley, he deplored the catastrophe that had come to his people, but like them he had slipped into an odd pattern of compromise. He slept in a wikiup utterly devoid of any of the white man's traps, and in whose smoky interior only the speech of his fathers ever was heard. For his labors he donned the white man's jeans, toiled the white man's way, and learned the white man's talk.

But the alert mind of Wovoka absorbed much more of the white man than just his speech or the ability to track behind a plow. The knowledge that tumbled in upon him, he cleanly divided into his mind's two compartments—the Indian and the white. He had never ceased to turn attentive ear to the past deeds and tribal lore of his people; he never lost an opportunity to absorb whatever knowledge was available from the white family among which he moved. He heard with two ears—but he weighed the facts, saw with sadness what was happening to his people, and secretly, almost ashamedly, wished that he had been born a white man like Jesus and the Wilsons.

The close comradeship which had grown up between Wovoka and the Wilson boys was prime cause of this racial tug-of-war. Through them he gained close insight into the white man's ways and thinking; his politics, religion, history and the avarice which made him a dangerous and ruthless foe. These friends, in turn became a sounding board to the young Indian's tribal experiences and yearnings. Bill, in particular, was a listener with sympathy and understanding. He never seemed to tire of the Paiute story, and plied Wovoka with questions concerning his life as an Indian, and the history of that proud, dark race whose interests were so inextricably intermingled in Mason Valley.

From Wovoka's lips, Bill Wilson heard the story of the Paiute's "big fight" at Pyramid Lake. White men called it a massacre. From Wovoka's lips, in Indian version, this last great struggle was a resounding victory over great odds and greater injustices.

A few years before Wovoka's birth a group of white miners had forcibly kidnaped the squaws belonging to some braves of the Paiute nation. These they mistreated, outraged, and imprisoned at Williams Station in Carson Valley. The grieving husbands gathered their friends, put on war paint, and rode against the whites. After liberating their women, the braves put the torch to Williams Station, and rode back to their people. The frightened miners fled to Virginia City and Washoe with tales of the raid. It grew in horror with every telling.

An army was raised among the miners to punish the Indians for their audacious assault. From Virginia City, Genoa, Carson and Silver City came volunteers for the punitive expedition. Under Major William M. Ormsby the army rode for Truckee, and northward toward Pyramid Lake. But the great Winnemucca had been apprised of the warlike moves of the whites, and, at the Truckee, was ready and waiting.

First thing Ormsby's men saw was a thin line of Paiute braves, riding a ridge, just out of gunshot, and ahead of them. The Major ordered a charge, and with wild whoops the white men rode forward to engage the enemy. The decoy had worked. From every side the Paiute braves arose, as if from the earth, and closed in. Major Ormsby, realizing his men had stupidly rode into a trap, ordered a retreat toward a high knoll which could make a possible defense. But it was too late. Panic had stricken his impetuous, untrained army, and he died pleading for the lives of his men. A few whites escaped, but most of them were cold-bloodedly hacked to death and scalped by Winnemucca's braves.

"It was the white man's fault," Wovoka told Bill Wilson. "Our people were always friendly toward your people before the big fight."

"Was there more fighting after that?" Bill asked.

"Much fighting," Wovoka said. "Many hates."

"But the white men finally won," reminded Bill.

And to this the young Indian could only passively agree. For only the Paiute, reduced to reservation and peonage, could know how utter and soul-destroying had been this defeat.

But organized resistance against the white invaders and despoilers had ended on an unforgettable note of defiance. In 1862 James Nye, territorial governor of Nevada, with the aid of Indian agent Warren Wasson, succeeded in negotiating a peace conference with the recalcitrant Winnemucca and his braves. The years had been bloody ones. The Ormsby massacre had been avenged with the slaughter of Paiutes by government troops at Pyramid Lake. And the soldiers at Fort Churchill had dealt with heavy hand upon all organized Indian resistance in Owens Valley. The white man was entrenched, never to be removed. The great Winnemucca, once friendly to the white man, but now thoroughly cornered, had no other alternative than to lay down his arms in defeat. The conference was held on the lower Truckee. Tävibo had attended, and Wovoka told his friend Bill Wilson the things his father once had revealed to him.

When the governor, Indian agent, and all the white man's soldiers arrived at the appointed place on the lower Truckee, near what became the white man's town of Nixon, they found Winnemucca, his sub-chiefs, and four hundred braves, all in battle paint and full regalia.

"Their big fire had burned all night," Wovoka told Bill, as the two of them lolled under a shading pine, and drank into their lungs the resinous scent of the highlands. "Much wood and sagebrush had been fed to the fire, until when the white men came it was a bed of glowing coals forty feet across, and hot enough to fry a rabbit down to the bones.

"When the white men rode in, my father raised his hand to the Sun God. Winnemucca lifted his voice in battle song, and jumped into the fire. The chant was raised by all the warriors. And while the governor and all his troops looked on in fright, the Paiutes danced their dance of war on the live coals. They never stopped until the fire went out."

"Didn't it burn their feet?" Bill asked.

"Of course it burned their feet—but no Paiute showed pain. My people sang their songs, cut their flesh with knives, and acted out their bravery—so that the white man would forever know the Paiute was no coward. That he was no woman in battle. That he was not afraid to die."

"But you said it was a peace conference."

"It was. And since that day the Paiutes have not painted for war. That day Paiutes put away their clubs and guns against the white man. But it was a day of sorrow, a day of hate, and no pipe of peace was smoked. It was a surrender all right, but one of which my father was proud. Chief Winnemucca told his people that fighting was no more. That all was hopeless. That white men now had their land, and white men were in numbers as the sands of the desert. There was nothing left but to weep in silence, and become as the white man."

Bill Wilson squinted his eyes and smiled at the young Indian beside him. "And so Wovoka became Jack Wilson—a white man."

"I wish Jack Wilson *had* been born a white man—like you. Then there would be no aches of sorrow inside my stomach."

"But you *are* a white man—practically," Bill remonstrated. "You work at a white man's house. You dress like a white man. You eat white man's food." Bill looked solemnly at the stocky Paiute youth, and thoughtfully toed the earth with his bare foot. "And don't forget," he said. "You're the best friend I ever had."

"But does that give me white man's blood?" Wovoka demanded fiercely. "I'm still Indian. I was born Indian. My blood's Paiute."

"Everybody calls you Jack Wilson," Bill insisted. "I say that makes you my brother."

"But my blood *is* Indian."

Bill thought a moment. His face brightened. He sprang to his feet. "I know how to fix it."

"Fix . . .?" Wovoka asked, rising.

"Fix your blood. I read about it in a book." Bill thoughtfully scratched his tousled, sunburned hair. "We'll do it up at the rock cove. Where you showed me the sacred medicine paint. We'll get Joe and George as witnesses. Come on." And Bill struck off at a fast walk through the mesquite and sage toward the house.

❀   ❀   ❀   ❀

While Joseph and George, the other two Wilson youngsters, looked on in fear and wonder, the little drama of blood-letting and blood-mixing was solemnly enacted in the granite cove where Tävibo and other Paiute mystics had for decades spooned out the sacred ochre for their ceremonies. By now Wovoka was aware of both implication and procedure, and willing enough to lend himself to the affair. Stoically he squatted on his hams while Bill methodically stroked the blade of his jack-knife to sharpness on a smooth boulder. Joe and George stood uneasily aside as the macabre preparations went on. On the rocky ledge behind them a ground squirrel chittered and scolded noisily at this invasion of his private hunting grounds.

Bill thumbed the blade for sharpness, wiped it on his pants-leg, and stood solemnly erect. Wovoka, in all the dignity of his race, arose, and took a waiting stance beside him.

"Oh, my brother, Jack Wilson—otherwise known as Wovoka—take this knife." Willingly the initiate accepted the blade. "Now draw my blood."

"Where?" asked the Indian.

"Here." Bill held out his right wrist. "One cut—and not too damned deep."

Quickly and efficiently Wovoka made a stroke across Bill's wrist with the blade. The two younger witnesses blanched with fear, and looked uncertainly at one another. Slowly, as Bill held his arm out, the crimson blood oozed in droplets to the surface.[4]

"Now I take the knife."

Dutifully Wovoka held out his own arm, while Bill, a little shakily, cut the darker flesh. The initiates, arms extended, watched silently while Paiute blood oozed forth. The squirrel continued to scold incessantly. Bill handed the knife to George.

"Now," said Bill at last, "as brothers in name, we become brothers in blood." Bill laid his bleeding wrist upon the red area of Wovoka's arm. "As my white blood enters yours, we become as one blood." Methodically they rubbed their bleeding wrists together. "From this day forward, I, Bill Wilson am your brother." He looked at Wovoka. "Now, you repeat the same."

"From this day forward I, Jack Wilson, am your brother," the Indian said.

Bill turned to the frightened youngsters alongside. "You repeat, 'And so witnessed.' "

"And so witnessed," they dutifully replied.

Bill smiled broadly and clutched his Indian friend by the arms. "Now you have white blood. You're all the same a white man."

Wovoka looked a little perplexed. Silently he turned and walked to the granite ledge. Here he paused, dampened a finger with spit, and ran it along the smooth red outcropping of ochre. Slowly he walked back, and, with the finger of red coloring, made a sacred mark on the forehead of Bill Wilson.

"You, too have my blood. You all the same my *Paiute* brother."

Bill scratched his head in new wonderment. That he might become a Paiute hadn't occurred to him. They both glanced at their blood-smeared wrists. Both laughed heartily and happily.

IV

THE GATES OF HEAVEN

My breath was out and I died . . . My soul left my body and went up to the judgment place of God . . . When I came back, I told my friends, "There is a God. My good friends, be Christians. If you all try hard and help me, we shall be better men on earth."　　　　　　　　　　　　—JOHN SLOCUM.

IT WAS easy enough to claim blood kinship with David Wilson's sons while they roamed the woods and river-bank as youthful playmates, and while the mystic fact was a secret known only to them. Eventually, however, time sorted them back to their original roles. With the arrival of first manhood, and young Bill Wilson started "mixing" at dances and socials, and playing closer heed to the young girls growing up in other Mason Valley's white families, there was less inclination to show off their more swarthy brother as true and presentable kin. Jack Wilson, of course, to the eyes of all other white families, was just plain Paiute, out of caste, and no blood-letting mysticism could ever make it otherwise. David Wilson, who would have held no brief with such nonsense, had he known about it, looked upon Wovoka as a brooding, gentle boy, inclined to be lazy and uncommunicative at times, but still no more than one Indian part of the peonage system the settlers had worked out in Mason Valley. Time itself had set Wovoka back into his inescapable role as Indian.

Too, as the son of Tävibo, more and more did the Walker River Paiutes show him the deference of his birth, gather him more deeply into the tribal councils, and indicate in every way they expected him to be something above the level of a white man's Indian. Wovoka, at first, was confused with this attention, and the conflict it made with his resolve to ape the white man in everything from dress to religion. He'd wanted to move through the world with the ease and assurance of a David Wilson, to learn all the white man's knowledge, and with this as power, step into some special greatness. But time brought its inexorable impact of racial barrier, and the bitter fact that white men, in the niceties of their civilization, did not consort with Paiutes. He'd always like, and be on friendly terms with, Bill Wilson and his brothers. But with time of manhood, there was no illusion. By destiny, and by birth, he was Paiute. He knew it, and the Wilsons knew it.

With this acceptance of an inescapable fact, it became easier for young Wovoka to ease into his tribal role,

WOVOKA, THE PAIUTE MESSIAH

Charcoal drawing from a photograph made on the spot by James Mooney, 1891.

—*Courtesy Bureau of American Ethnology.*

WOVOKA
From a postcard sold in drug stores and cigar counters of Nevada.

and even take a degree of pride in the fact that somehow his people expected special things from him. At the same time, it was heartbreaking to assess the servitude that had come to his people, and the poverty foisted upon them by the ruthless, land-grabbing white settlers. Their valley, once a green spot of peace and plenty, had now become the fenced domain of a race who looked upon the dispossessed with contempt. The Wilsons had always treated him with more consideration than did other white families for whom the poverty-stricken Paiutes labored for their pittances and their handouts. But time, withal, had brought Wovoka face-to-face with the fact that he was nothing special in the white man's eyes; that he could never truly aspire to their circles; that he was just plain Paiute.

In the smoke-filled wikiups of his people, Wovoka heard much that filled his heart with an ache that was never to leave him. He saw how useless was the bitter denunciation of the white man by his tribal elders, when he came to realize that the rape of Mason Valley was as nothing compared to what had occurred elsewhere. From one ocean to the other, the white man had slaughtered the Indian, driven the remnants of a once-great people into sterile reservations, and destroyed to the last animal the buffalo and all the once plentiful game that for centuries had given the Indian tribes their food, clothing, and shelter. It was hard not to be bitter, when he heard the telling of these things.

He saw, too, the degradation so manifest in the Indian defeat—drunkenness, debauchery, the whoring of squaws with whites, the fearsome and destroying diseases of lungs, skin, and the organs of sex. These things, which had sapped away the last will to resist, were made doubly hideous by the fact that they, too, had come from the white man. The coming of manhood to Wovoka was not the reckless, happy thing that it was to the sons of David Wilson. The impact of sorrow, the retrospection, and the soul-searching, turned Wovoka more deeply into an Indian. For two years he shunned his white brothers, and wrestled with a hate for the whole white race that all but consumed him. For two summers and two falls, instead of laboring for David Wilson, he joined a migratory group of Paiute young men from the Pyramid Lake reservation, who had permission to work as paid hands in the California, Oregon and Washington hop fields. The hop growers and truck farmers of these states had found in the Paiute a cheap and trustworthy source of labor, and they were increasingly in demand.[5]

The smugness and prosperity of the white man in Oregon and Washington impressed Wovoka no more than had the white usurpers of Mason Valley. His in-

terest now was all Indian, and in the soul-battle being
fought within him, he became the gentlest and most
understanding sort of counsel to his less retrospective
and more worldly Paiute working friends.

In these two years he came in contact with natives
from other tribes, particularly from the Squaxin, Nis-
qually, Skokomish, Chehalis and Yakima tribes. He
had difficulty with their languages, but his friendly and
observing interest gave him entry into their house-
holds. And whenever he was in the vicinity of Indians,
he paid these visits. His Paiute companions showed no
such interest. Whatever idle time they possessed was
well taken up in gambling, and the never-ceasing
search for the white man's firewater. In nearly every
instance Wovoka discovered the same defeatism, the
same vices, the same diseases preying upon the minds
and bodies of these diminishing tribes of the northwest
as he had found among the Paiutes of the Walker
River. One notable exception was his contact with a
family from the Skokomish tribe and their brief intro-
duction to him of the new and amazing faith of Squ-
sacht-un and Ai-yäl.

Squ-sacht-un, or John Slocum, as he was known to
the whites of southwestern Washington and northwest-
ern Oregon, had founded his religion only a few years
previously, but it had swept like a burning fire through

every Indian hamlet in the area.[6] Up to the time of Slocum's translation, he had been a common Indian, no different than any other colorless individual of the diminutive Squaxin tribe from which he originated. And he had been given to the usual drinking, horse-racing, and gambling so prevalent among his people.

One day John Slocum had been drawn into a state of deepest remorse, not only for his own sins, which were many, but for the sins of his people. In his earlier years he had come in contact with the Catholic religion, and later, had listened with interest to the Presbyterian missionaries who were active with the Indian population of that area. But these religious precepts had been abandoned with his childhood and, like most of the lazy reservation Indians about him, he had become addicted to the whiskey stealthily purveyed by the white traders, and all the debauchery and follies that accompanied it. But one October day he came face-to-face with these specters of evil, which had all but destroyed him and his people, and in deepest contrition, he went to the woods, and humbly knelt in prayer for forgiveness and strength. The wanted and needed strength did not come. Instead, he grew suddenly and violently ill. The sicker he grew, the brighter became his mind to the course and the duty now laid upon him with devastating clarity. But physically he grew steadily worse until, to all appearances he died. His body was laid out for burial. His brother went to Olympia for a coffin, and his grave was prepared. Suddenly, however, the corpse revived. John Slocum announced to his frightened and startled family and friends that his soul had been to heaven, that he had walked and talked with the angels of God, and that they had instructed him in the things he should tell his people.

The recovery of Squ-sacht-un was rapid. The zeal of his preaching increased enormously with the return of his physical health. His doctrine was a simple one— of complete abstinence from drinking, gambling, swearing, whoring, and all other major and petty vices of the white man. Constant prayer, humility, love, and the healing of the sick, were essential parts of the revealed religion.

What gave it peculiarity was the form this worship took. Crosses, signs of the cross, images, holy paintings, candles, and bells, were borrowed from the Catholicism which John Slocum had been briefly exposed to. Preaching fire and austerity were borrowed from the Presbyterianism in his recollection. The blowings, exorcism of spirits, trances, and body-quakings were holdovers from the pagan medicine and witch rituals of the Indians themselves. They crossed themselves like

Catholics; they said grace before and after meals; they prayed and chanted in unison; they set candles around the dead; they believed in the cure of the sick by faith and prayer. They professed a belief in God the Father, and in His Son Jesus Christ, as Savior of mankind. Heaven was a sure thing, for John Slocum had been there. And Hell was equally sure for sinners, because the angels themselves had made it known. They had little use for the Bible, because its revelations and prophecies were too ancient to be important, and because the Indian and his problems seemed to have been left out of its dogma and its promises. And anyway, through Squ-sacht-un, the heavens had been opened more directly and more recently to the poorest and the least of all the Indian tribes on earth.

Ai-yäl, or Louis Yowaluch, as he was more commonly known, was first convert, and with such conviction and energy that he immediately became high priest to the new church. Under the zeal of these two evangelists the Indians of western Washington forsook their sins and firewater, and flocked in great numbers into the new religion which offered immediate help and greater promises. Churches were quickly erected. To the sound of bells and chanted prayers, the converts swayed themselves into spiritual ecstasy, and they quaked and twitched with such violence that Slocum's new religion quickly became known as the "Shakers." Up and down Puget Sound, south into Oregon, and west into the Yakima country went Slocum, Yowaluch, or the numerous disciples "set apart" for the task. So successfully did Slocum and Yowaluch talk the new revelation, that they speedily and summarily talked themselves into jail. At the time Wovoka came in contact with the faith, its two spiritual leaders were languishing in a dirty little room of the jail at the Puyallup Indian Agency, near Tacoma. They had been arrested and confined at the instigation of the agent, Edwin Eells, and his brother, Rev. Myron Eells, a Christian missionary on the Skokomish reservation.

But jailing its leaders, and banning its public worship, had little effect on the new religion. In the homes and at the firesides of its members the chants, prayers, and healing rituals went steadily on. The peculiar twitchings, and mesmeric, vision-producing trances of the Shakers never ceased in the hundreds of little circles wherever Indians gathered. Its initiates crossed themselves whenever they met, brushed one another lightly with the fingers, to brush away evil and temptation, and blew upon one-another the holy breath of life. Tribal shamans and medicine men cast aside their outmoded Indian paraphernalia to accept the holy bells, holy candles, holy chants, and the hypnotic wonders they produced. Either they became blower doctors in the new faith, or spiritual leaders in the chants and rituals that sent its participants into twitching ecstasy, heavenly trances, or the cataleptic rigidity in which the body died for days at a time, and the spirit soared toward its celestial visit.

Wovoka penetrated the area of Squ-sacht-un's influence only far enough to take part in the household séances, with no opportunity to participate in one of its churches or public forms of worship. But even the little he saw made deep and lasting impression on a mind already hungering for hope, and to a heart groping sorrowfully for the answers. He saw the Shäpupulema, or blowers, as they entered the humble lodge, first gently wave hands in front of each other's faces like a fan, then blow on each other, to blow away the evil. He saw twelve of them gather around a sick man, each wearing a crown of woven cedar bark, upon which were affixed two lighted candles. In the left hand of each was another lighted candle, while the right hand carried the colored cloths of yellow, white or blue, with which, as shields, they changed the color of the lights in varied portions of the performance.

He watched in wonder while the priest fanned and blew the patient, and the twelve chanters swayed in unison with their candles over the sick one. The rhythmic dirge, the monotonous ringing of the bell, the swaying lights, and the close proximity of human bodies soon had profound effect not only upon the sick one, but on his viewers as well. The patient began to shake uncontrollably, and the chant became louder and more compelling. Soon the viewers squatting about the room began twitching with a strange and compelling ecstasy. Wovoka's own muscles began to ripple and quake, as drowsily he watched the moving lights and listened to the prayerful monotony of sound. Soon his head was hanging like a loose bag on his shoulders. The last he remembered were the shouts and convulsions of the patient from between the swaying priests. When he awoke, the congregation was gone, the sick one was stretched out in cataleptic rigidity on his blanket in the corner of the log hut. The only person seemingly alive in the room was his host's woman, whose head was still bedecked with time-wilted holy flowers.

She smiled when she saw him awake and stir himself. She went outside, and a moment later returned with a bowl of fish chowder. Over this she said a prayer in Skokomish, handed it to him, and then crossed herself reverently. She asked him, in her own dialect, something about whether he'd seen God. Wovoka made no attempt to answer, having no skill in her way of speech. He made ready to go, but before he did, he cornered his host outside, and learned that not only had he slept out an all-night trance, but that the sick one would awake from the dead in "maybe one day, maybe two days, maybe three days." And after this visit to heaven, he would be a well man.

Once or twice later in his life Wovoka was to come in contact with visitors from the northwest tribes, and emissaries from Slocum's Shaker religion. But two things he never forgot about that strange faith was its power to lift men out of the vices and sins that destroyed them as a people, and its ability to verily float a man's spirit out of his body. He never realized, at the time, how deeply he would some day borrow from it.

V

Worker of Great Wonders

*Do not refuse to work for the whites and do not make any trouble with them.
... When the earth shakes, do not be afraid. It will not hurt you.* —WOVOKA.

FROM that time forward, Wovoka was more content
to remain in Mason Valley. Every year the opportunity came to join the hop pickers and agricultural
crews which went out from the reservations to Pacific
farmers in quest of cheap and reliable help. Wovoka
had definitely decided his place was with his own
people, to stand with them in their own battle for sur-
vival, and to do all he could to lift them above their
present roles of ragged outcasts.

David Wilson hired him whenever Wovoka himself
felt the urge to work. His incipient hatred of the white
man had been rooted out by a new love of his Indian
heritage, and a strangely-formulated desire to con-
secrate his life, like Squ-sacht-un and Tävibo, to the
uplift and betterment of the Paiutes among whom he
lived, and to whom he owed a first allegiance. He had

no desire to essay the role of medicine man, which with his knowledge now of other healings, and his own family background, he would have been eminently fitted. Among Paiutes the position of medicine man was a precarious one indeed. When cures were effected, no man could bask in greater esteem and privilege. But let him fail in his role as healer, let a few patients die under his ministration, and he would just as quickly find himself put to death for his failures.

As son of a prophet and dreamer, he already possessed caste and deference in Mason Valley. There was no question that, among his people, something was expected of him. Yet the one role he coveted was not that of medicine man, but that of a mighty magician, a worker of wonders, like Jesus Christ, or maybe like Squ-sacht-un. There was, however, no urge on his part to establish a formal religion. Squ-sacht-un had tasted of what usually occurred when Indians rejected the white man's Christianity in favor of their own. And Jesus Christ had been killed when He started *His* church. No; death and jail were not for Wovoka—not at his age, anyway. Just a worker of wonders, that would be for him. A healer without the stigma of "medicine man" or its dangerous implications. Wovoka . . . magician . . . purveyor of the miraculous . . . doer of good.

His father had taught him many of the closely-guarded tricks of the shamans—the deft manipulation of hands, so as to make common objects like beads, coins and cards vanish and appear before the eyes of his viewers. He knew hat tricks, whereby objects seemingly leaped from one upturned hat to another. He had carefully been coached in all the songs of Paiute sorcery and healing. He knew the processes involved in the excorcising of spirits—both for good and for evil. To him had been revealed the precise healing virtues of various plants and the particular tissue portions or exudation of birds, insects and animals. No son could have been better qualified to follow in his father's footsteps. No man among the western Paiutes was better equipped to carry the medicine bags and bundles among his people. But, even though his tribal brethren already were pushing him into the role of medicine man, by bringing their sick to him for advice, he steadfastly refused to accept the precarious mantle of the mumbling and chanting healer. Sorcery, magic, the awe-inspiring voice of prophecy—those were the gifts and the callings he coveted beyond any earthly thing.

He arranged for séances in his little tulé wikiup. His audiences were always deeply impressed with the skill of his fingers and the deftness of his singing performances. They left him dressed rabbits and even money;

they talked much about what they had seen; but they elevated him to no particular greatness. He was still the son of Tävibo; not another, or greater, Tävibo.

Wovoka, realized that only by some spectacular demonstration of supernatural powers would he ever lift himself out of the role of wikiup magician onto the high seat of fame and esteem he coveted, and away from the dangerous and unwanted career of medicine man toward which his people seemed determined to push him. A great and wonderful feat of magic—like the bringing down of rain, or a shaking of the earth, was what he needed to impress upon his people that he had been born to a peculiar and spectacular destiny. All through the spring and into the summer he pondered this most necessary miracle, and his slender chances of ever achieving it. Not until late July did an idea sufficiently dramatic for his purposes, and still within the possibilities of his accomplishment, dream itself out of his inventive mind. When the great thought finally did germinate, he laid his plan with the skill and finesse of an impresario.

First he held a wikiup séance, and invited everyone to attend. In the crowded, smoky little room, he went over his repertoire of magical manipulation of feathers and objects, to set the stage of supernatural curiosity. When all were duly impressed, he faked a trance, like he had observed among the Shakers; even twitching a little, to add to the illusion. Then with eyes staring into the tiny fire, the unseeing eyes of a shaman in a trance, he quoted a line of Paiute sorcery. When all was still, and drama high, he went into the profundity of his announcement, speaking in the language of his people, with the stentorian voice of a real prophet.

"Tomorrow it comes. I see it. At the white man's bridge. At noontime it comes. The air is hot. The sky is hot. The sun he is hot. But you shall see. At white man's bridge. In summertime. In hot summertime. And you shall see what I see. It is ice. It is ice. Floating down river in hot summertime. You shall see."

There was talk, there was laughter, there was disbelief, when Wovoka's audience left the wikiup. But next day at noon, the white man's bridge was crowded with Indians. For a hundred yards up the river's banks stood the Paiutes, waiting either for the miracle to occur, or for Wovoka's seemingly impossible prediction to end in failure.

Wovoka was not unmindful that he had gambled everything on his ability to float ice down the Walker River in mid-summer. There was no doubt that should he fail, he would be discredited forever, and any hopes for greatness would vanish with this day's heat. He wiped the sweat from his flat, wide brow with his bandanna, looked upward at the sun in its high place, and with the dignity of a prophet, he pushed his way through the silent crowd to the bridge's center. There he methodically spread Tävibo's prayer blanket on the rail facing the fast-flowing river, and gazed a little nervously upstream.

"It's twelve," came the ominous reminder of the only Indian present with a watch.

Wovoka stared upstream for the tell-tale marks of floating ice. His heart galloped uncertainly, as he saw nothing but green water. With a hundred waiting eyes upon him he raised his arms toward the sun, and began his chant. For five minutes he sang in crying plea for the miracle his audience, with increasing impatience, were waiting to see.

Voices now began to heckle him. There was derision and laughter. But bravely he went on with his chanted prayer. After five more minutes of praying, the crowd commenced to get unruly. They had begun to call him a fake prophet. The sweat now stood out on his forehead. His long neck-length hair was wet with it. People were moving off the bridge, and away from the river bank. A little knot of Paiute braves had pushed closely around him. Wovoka knew that unless ice soon appeared on the Walker River, he would be unceremon-

SITE OF THE GHOST DANCE

At this place, in Mason Valley, Nevada, Wovoka revealed the doctrine of his religion to hundreds of Indians from all over America, and taught them the Ghost Dance as he had learned it during his visits to heaven.

—*Paul Bailey photo.*

WOVOKA AND COL. TIM McCOY

Photograph taken in 1926 during a visit of Tim McCoy to the almost forgotten Messiah. Mason Valley, Nevada.

iously heaved into its wet and discreditable depths. Frantically he shouted his song.

Stout Paiute hands were being laid on his shoulders and the seat of his pants. Much laughter was beating into his chant as they made ready to unceremoniously dump him into the deep. And then, at the bend of the river, upstream, he saw it. The chunks of ice were like white blinking eyes as they bobbed happily and fortuitously toward him. To save his own skin at this critical juncture, Wovoka let out a loud, triumphant howl, and stretched his arms exultantly toward the sun. Luckily, others had seen the ice. The hands, which a moment later would have heaved him into the drink, now dropped from him. Other hands were pointing frantically toward the bobbing ice as it drew closer toward the bridge. With a happy whoop, some of the younger men dove into the water, and grabbed the first chunks as they swept alongside. It was a moment of vindication and of triumph for Wovoka. Here was ice, miraculously floating in the Walker River, at noontime, and in summer. Here was a promised miracle accomplished. Here was a prophet made suddenly whole and real, by the sure test of prophecy—its fulfillment. Here was magic—by a recognized maker of magic. And in this one instant Wovoka knew his fame was assured, and every western Paiute would hear about the wonder of this day. He brought his arms, in dignity, to his sides. With all the austerity of his race, he strove to look like a prophet.

❋   ❋   ❋   ❋

And the Paiutes, pathetically credulous, made no request for explanation of the miracle, other than that the son of Tävibo had indeed used strong medicine this day. No other Indian but Wovoka was in possession of its secret. For that day Bill Wilson and his brothers had punctually aided in a miracle that for decades would be echoed up and down the river. The fact is, it was customary for the Wilsons and other Mason Valley ranchers to "put up ice" from the frozen lake in the winter, for use during the months of summer. Packed in sawdust, it kept well in log ice houses. Today, as a brotherly gesture to Jack Wilson, and as a sworn secret aid to his advancement in the tribe, they obligingly had dumped a wagon load of it into the stream.[7]

VI

Doo-mur-eye

Different writers have made him a Paiute, a half-blood, and a Mormon white man. —JAMES MOONEY.

HE was now twenty years of age, and his life star was in the ascendancy. His prestige and standing among his people were more than ever firmly secured, and his economic welfare flourished along with his rise. He took a comely young squaw to wife, in whose veins the blood of chieftains flowed, and promptly changed her Indian name to Mary—the name of Mrs. Wilson, whose gentleness and kindness toward him he had never forgotten. Surest recognition of his standing among the Walker River Paiutes was the fact that rabbits, venison, and all the products of their hunts were divided with their newly-risen prophet. The little tulé wikiup was never without food, and to the rabbit drives he rode in a wagon, drawn by horses; in dignity, and in state. He worked occasionally for the Wilsons, but more out of friendship than economic necessity. When they, or any other Mason Valley ranchers, desired Paiute labor, Wovoka now acted in the role of agent and procurer. And, if money were needed, he was entitled to demand a tithe of their earnings for himself.

Recognizing a good thing when he saw it, he steadfastly refused to accept the role of medicine man to his people. As dreamer and prophet he could dole out advice and guidance, wield extraordinary power, and, since he dealt in the mysteries, with nothing concrete or tangible, he could blame any failures on the vagaries of the gods and spirits he invoked. Or, in the case of failure of the human recipients to receive full measure or positive fulfillment, he could lay a proper blame on the petitioners, either for neglect to carry out properly their own part in the involved ritual, or for the fact that they themselves were under the cloud of divine displeasure. On the other hand, when a mere medicine man consistently failed at his healing, and his patients continued to die in spite of his ministrations, under Paiute custom, he was considered as evil, and divinely rejected. Promptly the hapless healer was put to death, so he might follow along with the patients who had died at his hands. Much as the sick and diseased Paiutes needed help, Wovoka stubbornly refused to broaden his talents in that direction.

But his talents in legerdemain were assuredly broadened in proportion to his rise. Edward Dyer, who knew Wovoka intimately, tells of one séance to which he was eye-witness. What the ritual was supposed to prove is obscure, but this again used ice, and was as dramatic as any in the Wovokan repertoire. Edward Dyer, young merchant in Mason Valley, and his brother Bob—both of them completely bilingual in Paiute— were alerted to the fact that some wonderful thing was going to happen among the tribesmen, and that in some way it concerned the prophet, Jack Wilson.

"Upon learning the time and place we unobtrusively showed up to see what was afoot," says Dyer. "The meeting took place along the river bank on a hot July day. A hundred or more Indians were present but there was no great excitement among them. Wilson was holding a sort of informal court at the side of a blanket spread upon the ground under a large cottonwood tree. Groups of Indians came up to talk to him and moved away. Other groups just milled around. We talked to some. They were distinctly not talkative to a white but we gathered that they expected Wilson to perform some miracle. Doo-mur-eye (accent on second syllable) they called it, which means an act of wizardry.

"Suddenly a great outcry came from the group around Wilson. Everyone rushed over to see what had happened. There in the center of the blanket lay a big block of ice, some 25 or 30 pounds in weight. Wilson had caused it to come from the sky, the Indians explained to those who had had their eyes turned the wrong way to see it for themselves.

"I was willing to believe that it had fallen all right, but from no greater height than the top of that cottonwood tree, whose dense foliage would serve to hide the object until sufficient had melted to release it from whatever ingenious fastening Jack had fashioned to hold it for a time. That explained why the type of miracle was unspecified in advance. No Indian was likely to look up into the tree as he might if he were expecting ice from Heaven. It also explained the blanket. No Indian would stand on Jack's blanket and perhaps receive a pre-miracle icy drip, or worse, be beaned by the chunk itself. The Indians, not being of my suspicious nature, accepted the miracle in full faith. A wash tub was provided from somewhere, the ice placed in the tub, the tub on the blanket and as the ice melted the ice water was ceremoniously drunk. It might have been sacramental wine to judge from the solemnity. Shortly thereafter, at Jack's order, the whole bunch stripped and plunged into the river. It wasn't until years later that I realized I had witnessed an aboriginal distortion of communion and baptism inspired by biblical tales imperfectly understood."[8]

In his heart Wovoka sensed shame for the quackery and trickery he had used to gain standing, and for the necessity of its continued use to hold himself in honor before his tribe. He wanted, more than anything on earth, to help lift his people above the degradation and poverty he saw on every hand. The prayers he offered from his wikiup, or in the holy places of the hills, were sincere and real enough. And the counseling and preaching that fell from his lips, as to the necessity for sobriety and the shunning of the white man's vices, had within it the elements of wisdom, and backed by a deep and living concern for those who now looked up to him with childlike faith. From Mary and David Wilson he had heard enough of the gentle teachings of Jesus to expand them into his own Paiute liturgy. A devout Christian would have looked on in either horror or amusement at the strange manner he mixed doctrine with the age-old paganism of his heritage. But in this new thing they were hearing from their new prophet there was enough bedrock wisdom and spiritual uplift to give the groping Wovoka a tool of strength. Mixed with the incantations and the hand-magic in which he was adept, was the personal sincerity of his feelings and his prayers. The aura of good, and the aura of mystery which clung to his presence, was enough to hold him secure in his office.

But with his fame spreading, it was not without difficulty and hazard he kept his standing. Gold was being discovered in the Pine Grove area, and the Wilsons, who were pioneers of the land, were as anxious as any of the other white settlers to come into their share of the riches. Bill Wilson, now also married, and living with his bride at Pine Grove, had laughingly asked Wovoka to use his gift of divination in the location of a worthwhile claim. After much prayer, a period of fasting, and some sober meditation, the spirit whispered out a likely location, and Wovoka conveyed the momentous news to his white brother. Bill went industriously to work at the site the unseen spirits had chosen. But this time the spirits were definitely wrong. The promised vein of ore refused to show itself. Bill shamelessly laughed the Paiute prophet into derision among the white men of the valley.

The prophet retired to his wikiup and brooded over his failure, and the abrupt way he had been dumped in white esteem. It was the mockery he had received from the smug and well-fed white men for his honest and prayerful attempt to help, that now etched itself into his sensitive skin. More than anything he wanted Bill Wilson to accept him, as the Paiutes had accepted him. More than any man living did Bill Wilson now know he was a fallen prophet and a fake. For weeks, in bitterness, he thought on the subject. Then one day, he approached Bill once more.

"This time I will show you gold," he promised. "Other time spirits were wrong. This time you shall see with eye. You will not have to dig."

"Jack," said Bill Wilson, "you show me an outcropping of ore, and you'll get paid for it. And I'll forget that other time when your spirits were wrong."

"You'll pay me twenty dollars?" asked Wovoka, smiling broadly.

Bill, surprised at the modest request, chuckled. "Hell, yes, I'll pay you twenty dollars! Just you show some gold to me."

An hour later Wovoka had his white brother before the ledge. And this time there could be no doubt that there *was* gold. It glistened tantalizingly from the gray rock wall. In an instant Bill Wilson sensed this as indeed a rich find. He insisted on paying Wovoka the twenty dollars before he could change his mind.

Back in his wikiup, with the now-pregnant Paiute Mary serving him roast rabbit, Wovoka wondered hopefully if what Bill received would somehow restore his standing among the whites. There was only one disconcerting note about the whole affair, a thing which he prayed time and discovery would not too harshly equate. Fact was that Bill Wilson would never take more than twenty dollars worth of gold from his mine. That was the amount of gold dust Wovoka had purchased, and with which he had used to load the shotgun shells. By firing the gun against the rocky wall, he had efficiently and handsomely distributed the rare metal in a most believable and appetizing pattern to the eye. It had never occurred to Wovoka that in choosing granite in which to deposit his gold, he was selecting a type of rock that nature herself had never before chosen.[9]

Bill Wilson quickly learned all this when he called in his friends to view his new and wondrous find. He never quite forgave Wovoka for the thing that he had done.

✣   ✣   ✣   ✣

As if the spirits themselves were weakly protesting this handling of his white brother, Bill Wilson's first child lived and grew healthy, while Wovoka's first baby was delivered stillborn. Twice more, as the snows and summers passed, Mary delivered dead babies, and Wovoka began to wonder if this woman would ever give him the son for which every man had the right to expect.

During this time he was not without visits from Slocum's disciples. The Shaker church, now freed from persecution by the northwest Indian agents and jealous missionaries, was prospering, and, strangely, had been taken under the protective wing of the Presbyterian council. The fame of the Walker River prophet, whether justly earned or not, had come to the Shakers. Wovoka welcomed the blower doctors into his lodge, learned considerably more about their trance-producing ritual, but rejected their church as the spiritual voice of his people. For the first time he had learned how to summon this deep sleep upon himself. But the religious custody of the Walker River Paiutes he had no intentions of sharing with any other man or group. Wovoka was convinced that the healing phase of Slocum's faith, if accepted by him, would cast him too closely into the hazardous role of tribal medicine man.

And from the east came another peculiar religious influence among the Paiutes who looked to him for guidance. Hundreds of the Paiutes of Utah and eastern Nevada had been dipped in water by the Mormons and had become pious members of that great white man's church. Mormons promised the Paiutes much. They had a book which was said to have been written by the ancestors of all Indians. They had promises that someday the Indians—that is the Mormon

Indians—would become white, like that church's missionaries who labored so diligently among them. Many of the eastern Paiutes had prospered, lived in houses and had risen so high in that church that they had visited its temples, and wore its holy underwear which protected its wearers from all bodily harm. They were now just as assiduously proselyting among the Paiutes from Pyramid Lake south.

There were phases about this Mormon church which interested Wovoka. The idea of achieving white man's status and color was not without its merits. And donning a garment which protected one from death and danger would be an impressive adjunct to one's magic. The book, too, would be an interesting thing to peruse—especially so if one were only able to read. And if it were written by the ancestors of the Indians, it should be a valuable help in resolving the problems and conflicts which plagued the poor Indian of today. But the very fact that all these things had been given into the custody of the already cruel and privileged white man, was enough to turn any thinking Indian away from it. With all its enticements he summarily rejected Mormonism.[10] If the eastern Paiutes wanted to embrace this faith, let them. But along the Walker River, where he alone stood as prophet, he wanted none of his people spiritually subservient to any organization run by white men. He frowned upon every visit of the Mormon elders. He counseled the turning of a deaf ear to their talk. And one woman, who was foolish enough to be dipped by them, was brought to him. He spent three nights chanting prayers for her fallen soul, and blowing away the evil that had entered her.

If the Paiutes of Mason Valley were in need of a prophet, he, a Paiute himself, was that man. He was determined there would be no other.

VII

THE HEAVENS OPEN

When the sun died, I went up to heaven and saw God and all the people who had died a long time ago. God told me to come back and tell my people they must be good and love one another, and not fight, or steal, or lie. He gave me this dance to give to my people. —WOVOKA.

ONE night while staring into the fire, and deeply contemplating the condition and problems of his people, the great sleep suddenly came upon him. When Mary found him, his massive head had sagged between his knees, and his body was as rigid and as cold as a day-old death. Only with greatest difficulty was he straightened out like a corpse upon his blanket.

Many were the visitors to his lodge in the anxious days that followed. Some thought him dead; others argued that he was alive and "with God." Frantic attempts were made to revive the sleeping prophet. Water was poured over him. Food was forced into his mouth. Breath was blown into his lungs. Flame was applied at his feet until the flesh burned and smelled, but still the prophet lay rigid and cold within his hut.

Had he been any less than Wovoka, son of Tävibo, he would have been buried along with lesser Paiutes. Because of this, and in spite of those skeptics who insisted he was truly dead, there was hushed expectancy that Wovoka would again stand among them in life.

Two days later the color began returning to the stocky young body, and before nightfall Wovoka had again opened his eyes upon the mundane world. From that hour on the prophet was a changed man. He touched no food until the next day. Reverently, insistently, he declared he had visited the other world. That he had talked to the spirits of his people's dead, and that they had taught him much.

The clamor became incessant for him to reveal to others the miracle which his spirit eyes alone had seen. After promising that he would tell of his heavenly sojourn at a dance the following night, he cleared the lodge of Mary and his visitors, and rocked himself in continuous song and prayer until the hour of his public revelation.

The Paiutes of Walker River needed no persuasion to attend this dance. Before excluding his visitors, Wovoka had chosen the dance area, a few miles southwesterly from the white man's settlement in Mason Valley. To the tribal elders he had given precise instructions as to its location, and as to how the brush ceremonial shelters should be built. News of Wovoka's death-trance, and the promised revelation, spread across the valley like ripples across the great lake. A steady stream of Paiutes flowed into the tree-rimmed flat which, unknown to that first excited gathering, was to become a peculiar center of destiny to the Indians of North America.

Wovoka rode to the ceremonial ground in fitting state—shrouded in blankets, high on a wagon, behind which walked Mary, his squaw. When the wagon lurched onto the flat, he saw with solemn eyes, that every Paiute in the area was present. In him this time there was no sense of exuberance or personal triumph. Born with the immensity of his vision, was the conviction and the surety that he truly was a prophet. He, if he wanted to, could discard his previous trickery like an earth-soiled shirt. At last, and as he'd always sensed he would be, he was a chosen one. And when, in this hour, he stood majestically among his people, he was aware in an instant that they sensed it also.

For one solemn hour Wovoka, with tears streaming down his face, expounded the wonders of his vision. He had been to heaven. In a mystic land of great beauty, in which all the once-savage elements had been subdued and glorified, he had walked and talked with the spirits of the departed. There he saw the savagery of the wild beast reduced to the tranquility of lambs at play. He saw all Indians, of every diversity, and of every nation, walking arm-in-arm as brothers. He saw the flowering of physical beauty, the end of all pain and all disease, and man's final victory over death. And there the Indian was not the slave and the beaten dog of the white man, but stood in gloried dignity and equality with all. At the feet of these exalted beings, he had listened with reverence and with awe.

"Go back to your people," they had counseled after Wovoka had pleaded to remain in this land of beauty and of peace. "Go back, and tell your people the things that you have seen, and the things that you shall hear. You must teach that Jesus is upon the earth. That He moves as in a cloud. That the dead are all alive again. That when their friends die, they must not cry. That they must not hurt anybody, or do harm to anyone. They must not drink whiskey. They must not fight. They must do right always. They must not refuse to work for the whites, and not to make troubles any more with them. You must take the dance we will show you back to earth. It is the dance of goodness. It comes from heaven. It has a purpose. It will make your people free, and it will make them glad."

Then carefully, and with the most meticulous attention to detail, Wovoka showed his people the dance which heaven had sent to them. Unlike most Indian dances, Wovoka chose both men and women to form this, the first circle of a dance that was destined to sweep into history. On their faces he painted some unknown signs with the red ochre he had brought with him. Facing the dancers inward, he joined hands with them, with fingers intertwined, so as to form them into a circle. In a soft undertone he commenced to sing; and then carefully coached the participants in the song. By that time darkness had settled deeply over the flatlands and mountains of Mason Valley. The stars, countless millions of them, had sharpened themselves into the light of night, and the great fire alongside was crackling and flinging its sparks and flame into the sky.

Not until the song was learned, and could be sung with confidence did Wovoka start the circle moving, from right to left. The step was simple, and stately. Scarcely lifting the left foot from the ground, it was advanced a step, with the right foot following into its spot, in unison with the song. Slowly the ring revolved.

When these first dancers knew their parts with proficiency, the circle was much enlarged, until a hundred candidates were sharing the experience, and the song had swelled to the throaty chorus of its many participants. New songs were taught by the inspired prophet. And for five successive nights the dance was repeated. This was followed by one afternoon performance, after which, at Wovoka's insistence, all participants dipped themselves into the Walker River, to wash their sins away, and make themselves pure before God and all the spirits gone before. After this, the community's meager food supply was appropriated, and a feast of spiritual peace was shared by all.

And for two peaceful years the shuffling circles of Wovoka's dance became familiar sights wherever Paiutes congregated along the western borders of Nevada. With the dimming of time came the scoffers and the skeptics to question and belittle the prophet's religious experience, but stolidly he clung to the story of his translation; that he had, in very deed visited the spirit world; that the full substance of his gentle and Christlike teachings had their inspirational beginnings in the heaven he had visited. Against his admonishments there were still Paiutes who bought whiskey at the white man's settlement, and drank themselves into destructive frenzy. There were still Paiutes in the sound of his voice who gambled away their substance, and who peddled their squaws in whoredom to the whites. But, in general, Wovoka's people listened respectfully to his teachings, and no man could deny that for days he had laid as one dead.

The Heavens Open

After his great soul-shaking experience in catalepsy, Wovoka found the trance-state easier to produce, not only in himself, but in others. With the eagle feather, which became his badge of divinity, and the magpie tail-feathers he distributed to his neophytes as optical targets in his ceremonies, he found that he now had the tools which had built Smohalla, Squ-sacht-un, and a dozen other great Indian dreamers into fame and influence. In the trance-state, it was possible to will and suggest what the participant would see, and amazing indeed were the religious experiences his low, vibrant voice and his feathers were able to conjure into the consciousness of those who sought his counsel.

He had no need now for trickery or illusionary skill to keep himself in influence. He had no need, either, to work in the white man's fields, as did other Paiutes. He asked no alms, but his lodge was always plentifully supplied with food, and those visitors who did not leave venison, rabbits, or piñon nuts, left money, which was even more acceptable. And yet, since a great point of his doctrine was the necessity of cheerful acceptance and endurance of the white man's burden, he set himself up as example by occasional work stretches with the Wilsons, or other white ranchers of Mason Valley. And, as though heaven itself were smiling, Mary's new child, a boy, had lived.

So it was, that about two years after his great religious experience, he accepted a winter assignment at Pine Grove for David Wilson. Mary packed the wagon with food and bedding, hitched up the horses, and they started south toward the scene of their labors. The snow was heavy at Pine Grove, so Wovoka built a shelter of pine boughs, and his sharp axe and heavy muscles were soon at work cutting the logs for which David Wilson had hired him. On the second morning he was so ill he could scarcely rise from his blanket. In concern Mary felt his face. It was hot with fire, and red as its embers. The prophet made another attempt to rise to his labors, but fell back weakly to his bed. His ears were hearing rumblings from the sacred mountain. He was a sick man.

In haste and fright, Mary took off for the river and the Indian settlement, astride one of the horses, and carrying her baby. A white man, riding the ridge, came upon the lonely wikiup in the snow. He dismounted, and peered in. What he saw was another Paiute with scarlet fever, and he beat a hasty retreat. An hour later Mary was telling her neighbors at the river about Wovoka having been struck down by sickness, and a delegation, headed by Wovoka's uncle, Charley Sheep, returned with her to the little shelter at Pine Ridge.

But the dispersal of Wovoka's friends was complete and hasty when they saw that their prophet was red with a white man's disease. None of them would risk his own life to lift the now delirious Wovoka into the wagon. In the end, Charley Sheep, with Mary's help, finally got their stocky prophet into the vehicle and, with Mary driving, and Charley Sheep following at safe and respectful distance, the stricken man was hauled back home.

In the cold weeks that followed, Wovoka fought his battle for life almost alone. Only Mary entered the lodge itself. Paiutes would not go near it. The Wilsons, and another rancher or two, left food at the door, and inquired solicitously of Mary regarding the delirious victim within. Wovoka himself was never to have recollection of what occurred during his bout with death.

When he did awaken to rationality, he was as weak as a dying trout. When Mary told his people that the dangerous color had subsided, and that her husband could once more see and hear again, the neighbors again found courage to enter the lodge. Their caution had been born out of wisdom. The disease had hit many during this snow. Unlike Wovoka, most of the other victims had died.

But, just as Wovoka had begun taking on food and enjoyment at the sight of his friends, and they in turn were beginning to attach a divine significance to the fact that their durable prophet had survived, then came that terrible, never-to-be-forgotten event—the death of the sun.

It was the first day of January. The morning had come in with a brightness and a warmth that would have melted the snow and turned the day to a time like spring. After saying his prayers to the day and its sunshine, Wovoka had felt well enough to crawl from his rabbit-skin blankets and peer outside at the immensity of blue and white, which was the sky and earth. Good as it seemed, he could not long stand the welcome scene, for his weakened eyes watered at the brightness, and his heart thumped in his ribs at the exertion. But, he felt well enough to eat, and called to Mary for food.

But even as he finger-spooned the piñon nut gruel into his mouth, the first haze of the eclipse, like the passing of a cloud between sun and earth, shadowed the great outside. But no one paid it any attention—leastwise the prophet, busied with his food and with his thoughts. By imperceptible degrees the gloom spread itself across the face of the land. Now Paiute eyes turned skyward, with anxious thoughts of another approaching storm. But there were no clouds. Not until a more discerning eye discovered the black shroud across the side of the sun's face, did the implication and meaning of the mid-day gloom assert itself in the understanding of the Paiutes.

For to them, the sun is a living being—a great, beneficent thing alive, which warms and lights the earth, and is receptive to prayers and incantations. To them, this encroaching eyelid of black, was the first move of some obscene sky-monster, intent on devouring the sun. Should any such death of the sun occur, the world forever would be plunged into black night. It was a terrible thing to contemplate. The man who had discovered this battle in the sky, let out one short, hideous scream, dove into his wikiup, and came out with an ancient and battered shotgun. This he pointed to the sky, and fired.

With shouts and screams, the alarm spread. More guns were fired. The word of catastrophe was spread from lip to lip. The monster must be frightened away. The sun must be saved.

What a moment ago had been a quiet and peaceful mid-morning, was suddenly turned into a pandemonium of howling men, wailing women, and the incessant din of drums, kettles, and gunfire. But in spite of heroic measures, the earth grew darker minute by minute, and the monster continued to bite greater and greater chunks out of the once-friendly sun.

Wovoka, weak and helpless, had heard the beginning of the din. Not until Mary's wail of despair outside, and Charley Sheep had burst into the lodge, did the stricken prophet realize that calamity had struck the earth. With Charley's frantic shouts of "The sun is dying!" Wovoka took first cognizance of the fact that the day had quite suddenly turned to twilight.

The hideous din outside increased. More frantic people were at his bedside beseeching his help in this awful hour. One of them shoved the sacred eagle's feather into his hand. He sat himself weakly erect, and began chanting the sun-prayer with all the fervency he possessed. But in spite of the noise, the gunfire, the wails, and the prayers of their prophet, the earth grew darker, and the sun relentlessly was bitten away by the monster.

With every darkening moment the Paiutes grew more frantic in their efforts to scare the monster away. But nothing prevailed. Evil was triumphant. Soon the blackness of total night had shoved out the glory of the day. Never did Wovoka pray with more sincerity, or with more fear.

With the complete and total death of the sun, the gunfire ceased, the shouts and drumbeats lost their notes of hope, and turned to human wails of utter despair. For an hour the Indian world mourned the tragic demise of their greatest, most beneficent friend. And then, from the very side from which the monster approached, there came a faint glimmer of light. It widened, and with its widening, the more hopeful cries burst out anew. Another gun was fired, drums again started sounding. Women again commenced beating on their cooking pots.

As the light of heaven slowly came back to Mason Valley, the tempo of the noise increased. Frantically every Paiute now did his utmost to frighten into complete rout that evil thing in the sky, And at long last success was completely theirs. Their noise had done a miracle this day. In elation they burst into the lodge of their prophet. Wovoka again was stretched out as though dead.[11]

VIII

DANCING DISCIPLES

You must not fight. Do no harm to anyone. Do right always.   —WOVOKA.

WOVOKA'S awakening from the dead was only a matter of days, but physical recovery from the depletion of disease was a slower process. That he had again seen visions, few doubted. The very hour of his translation had been a climactic one. To be ushered out of mortality in the awful moment of the sun's death, had all the portents of divine timing and celestial intervention. And the credulous Paiutes, after ascertaining with fire and knife on Wovoka's seemingly lifeless flesh that it was no ordinary sleep, were ready enough to ascribe the sun's escape from the black monster to the high assistance of their heaven-borne prophet. When Mary, and the tribal elders, plied the wasted but bright-eyed Wovoka with the question of where he had been, and received in turn the simple answer of "with God," it was enough. Their prophet had again been favored. When he spoke—and it would be in his own due time—

it would be as thunder rolling off the holy mountain. Great things could be expected. And while they waited, they nightly danced in the pattern Wovoka had revealed to them.

Nor were they disappointed when the prophet finally was physically able to stand before them and speak his mind.

"I have talked to God," he said simply. And never, as long as he lived, was any man ever to hear him deny or water down this statement.

What God had told, became the substance of Wovoka's new revelation to his people.

"Pretty soon now, the earth shall die," Wovoka revealed to his eager listeners. "But Indians must not be afraid, because earth will come alive again. Just like sun died and came alive again."

It was what would occur during and after the great transition which became important not only to the Paiutes of Mason Valley, but to the spiritually broken and defeated Indians everywhere. "Earth will shake like a dancer's rattle. Thunders will come—and smoke— and great lightning. For the earth is old, and it must die. But Indians must not be afraid. It is the whites who must be afraid." The Indian dead had all arisen, he told his startled people. "They are waiting, in the place where the sun rises. With them is the spirit captain, who moves like a cloud, and Old Man [God]."

In that hour when the earth would begin to shake, all Indians who were faithful and understanding of the prophecy, must gather in the high country to watch and await the earth's death, and translation into life. Most impressive thing in Wovoka's revelation was the promise that the white race, along with all Indian skeptics would be cleanly wiped off the earth's surface by a mighty flood of mud and water. After this dramatic demise of their oppressors, the Indian would become young again, free of disease and pain, and the land would once more become green with high, luxuriant grass. The game, including the vanished buffalo, antelope and elk, would return in primeval abundance, and everything earthwise would be an Indian paradise, "just like the old times."

All faithful Indians would have a very definite part in bringing these wondrous things to pass. They must "Do no harm to anyone," Wovoka said, in reiteration of his original doctrine. "You must do right always. You must not tell lies. You must not fight—not even against the white man—for The Old Man will take care of him. And when your friends and your family die, you must not cry. For they are alive, and I have seen them." The earth's great renewal would come only if Indians practiced these basic tenets and, just as important, danced, five nights at a time, the great sacred dance Wovoka already had taught his people.

The rise in Wovoka's divine stature by this dramatic visit to the spirit world was indicated by the fact that God had made him custodian of the elements. Five new songs had been given to him, most efficacious in the making of rain. One song, when properly executed by the prophet, brought on a mist or cloud; the second one had to do with a snowfall; the third a shower; the fourth would miraculously fetch a hard rain, or even a cloudburst; and the fifth song would clear the skies, and bring out the sun. Another important confession to his people was the fact that God had now made him invulnerable. "Even if soldiers should try to kill me, they will fall down, as if they had no bones, and die," he modestly promised. "I would still live, even if they cut me into little pieces."[12]

The transformation of St. Paul, and the religious experience he passed on to the gentiles, were as nothing compared with the spiritual fervor Wovoka's revelation awakened among his Paiutes. In light of what it could do to hasten the world's redemption, his dance took on new import and new significance. People now gripped his pudgy, work-calloused hand, and called him "Our Father." In consideration of his messianic divinity, those seeking his wisdom and his counsel, now met him with averted eyes, lest this Paiute Jesus shrivel them in their sins with a single piercing glance. Some of the more fanatic ones, equally desirous of a round-trip to heaven, tried every means known to them to produce the catalepsis by which Wovoka had died and come alive before their very eyes. Unsuccessful in their attempts to mechanically produce the necessary deep trance, they turned to a surer way—the eating of wild parsnip root (water hemlock). It quickly produced the desired death-state. Whether those who partook of it ever saw God, or visited the Indian spirits so anxiously waiting to invade the earth, it was never learned. Unlike Wovoka, the silent ones never awakened to tell their story.[13]

While the dancing and spiritual purification went on in Mason Valley and the Pyramid Lake and Walker Lake reservations, the fame of the new Messiah spread rapidly to the north and to the east. Here was the greatest Indian prophet who ever lived, with a message of universal significance, a promise to all Indians, far transcending the minute little Paiute circle of Mason Valley, Nevada. In a matter of months the Washoes, the Bannocks, and the Pit Rivers were moving in the stately, shuffling circles of Wovoka's dance—or the "ghost dance," as the white man began to call it—while they practiced the virtues of his doctrine and waited with anxious hearts and eyes the transformation of the world. Paiute apostles carried the new tidings to the Walapai, Cohonino, Mohave, and the far-off Navajo. Even the Mormon-evangelized eastern Paiutes, and the Utes of the Great Basin area, began learning the new dance, and listening with attentive ears to the great tidings now coming out of the west. No religious movement in history ever swept with greater speed or more dramatic impact across the face of the land. For the first time in two hundred years of death and oppression, a voice of hope and promise was raised to the dwindling, beaten tribes of North America. Wovoka himself could scarcely have realized that his simple, unlearned words and convictive declarations would, in a matter of months, blow themselves into a whirlwind.

Magpies and eagles were trapped and plucked for the ceremonial feathers. Ochre was dug from the vicinity of Mount Grant, the holy mountain of the Paiutes, mixed with water, and dried into cakes—the red paint so spiritually essential to the dance itself. These consecrated objects, passed by "Our Father"[14] himself to the visiting emissaries, went out to other tribal areas and became requisites essential to the spiritual link with its source, and the proper observance and functioning of the ghost dance.

The eastern segment of the Paiute nation, spiritually dominated by the Mormon Church, more than ever turned acute ears to the sensationally new doctrine which had erupted as a living flame out of the area of Walker Lake. For one thing, redemption of the American Indian was a basic tenet of this faith. The *Book of Mormon,* that unique scripture said to have been dug out of a New York hill, in the form of graven gold plates, and translated with divine assistance by their prophet, Joseph Smith, was an historical record of the American Indian and his predecessors upon the American continent. In this book, as widely accepted by the converted of the eastern Paiutes as it was by the white Mormons themselves, held forth the promise that the earth would undergo a physical transformation, that the faithful would be gathered out of all the lands of the earth, that the American Indians would be lifted out of their barbaric state, and would become again the "white and delightsome" people which their *Book of Mormon* ancestors had claimed to be. The physical curse upon this unhappy race would be lifted, and they would step forth into a reclaimed world in all the beauty of a God-favored people.

The Book told of how the Christ had once visited the American continent, set up His church, and had chosen twelve favored disciples from among the natives. In the Book was the heartening promise that this same Messiah would again return, and personally hasten the redemption of a race, which the Book claimed had its genetic origin in ancient Judea.

Mormonism had not made too much headway in the western segment of the Paiute nation, principally because of the opposition of the American settlers and mining men along the eastern base of the Sierra Nevadas. Once Mormons had claimed all of Carson Valley, with a flourishing settlement at Genoa, but their hopes and holdings had dwindled when Brigham Young, in 1857, had called back the faithful to Salt Lake Valley. At that time Johnston's Army was hammering at the gates in the "Utah War." Yet here, from a strangely unexpected quarter of the Paiute nation, was a messianic prophet risen. His message and his promises bore close semblance to those of Mormon doctrine. Converted Paiutes by the scores saw in Wovoka not only God's working means for their rejuvenation and redemption, but they quickly claimed him as their own.

The circles of the ghost dance began forming in the very shadows of the Mormon chapels. Mormon white settlers themselves, cognizant of a familiarly ringing religious phenomenon in their midst, listened attentively to the new tidings, and before long they themselves were shuffling in the dance circles along with their "Lamanite" brethren of the promise.

With a dozen western tribes already spiritually afire, the flame of the new and compelling religion swept eastward. The great prairie nations were hearing rumors of a prophet who miraculously was lifting the Indian heart out of despair. Beaten and humiliated by the white man beyond any words of description, the buoyant hope voiced by an Indian himself, was something to be heeded for whatever it was worth. Poverty, degradation, defeat and despair, had already made the field white and ready for the harvest. Wovoka, in the day he uttered his new revelation, could not have remotely imagined how hungry was the Indian world for his words, or how fast and how far they were destined to travel.

IX

The Ghost Dance Goes East

I found my children were bad, so I went back to heaven and left them. I told them that in so many hundred years I would come back to see my children. At the end of this time I was sent back to try to teach them. My father told me the earth was getting old and worn out and the people getting bad, and that I was to renew everything as it used to be and make it better. —WOVOKA,

THE FIRST great dance, in which Wovoka perfected his people in its new intricacies and spiritual concept, was performed in January 1889, a short mile above the railroad bridge, and not far from the Walker Lake agency headquarters.[15] There were few if any visitors from outside tribes at this prime scene of the great revelation. Subsequent dances, held in a meadowed area in the upper end of Mason Valley, within a few miles of the the Mason Valley Post Office (later to become the town of Yerington, Nevada), had brought eager disciples from dozens of western tribes who previously would scarcely have given the humble Paiutes a second thought. Before summer the throbbing, shuffling circles of dancers had become a yearning and eager composite of tribes and remnants of tribes within a thousand mile radius. Dignified Navaho and taciturn Utes held hands and rubbed shoulders with rebellious Apaches and submissive Bannocks. All had journeyed far to look upon the face of the man who had visited heaven and to hear firsthand the inspired words which fell from his lips. The things they learned, and the carefully rehearsed ritual of the dance, were soon carried back to their own peoples.

And before the year was out Wovoka, either by design or the insistent processes of human deification, had emerged from Paiute prophet to Indian Messiah and finally to the inviolate Christ. By the time the plains tribes began their hungry investigation of the new doctrine, Wovoka had risen to such spiritual stature that his visitors approached "Our Father" with awe, reverence, and averted eyes, lest they be shriveled and burned at his presence.

During summer and fall of 1889 the first investigators from the great plains tribes had carried back the wondrous story of the new Messiah, and by fall the Indian nations from the Rockies to the Mississippi River were cognizant of the strange miracle taking place in the Far West. In November of that year a delegation crowned with all the dignity and respect of an investigative commission arrived in Mason Valley from those faraway tribes to the east. It was headed by Porcupine, representing the Cheyennes; Short Bull and Kicking Bear, from the Sioux nation; and delegates from the Bannocks and Shoshones. The things they saw and learned were eagerly accepted. They were forerunners of many other delegations from the East, and the first firm bridge across the Rockies for the ghost dance and the doctrine of the New Messiah.

The Indian Office and War Department, alarmed by the dancing frenzy sweeping America, took Porcupine into custody some months later. Major Henry Carroll, commanding officer at Camp Crook, Tongue River agency, forced a candid statement out of Porcupine, and transmitted it to Washington, D. C. The clarity, honesty, and simple dignity of Porcupine's story of his visit to Nevada should name him the Apostle Paul to the new movement. But, like his counterpart of old, the strange tidings he bore stirred up rumblings in Rome.

"In November last I left the reservation with two other Cheyennes," said Porcupine. "I went through [Fort] Washakie and took the Union Pacific railroad at Rawlins.[16] We got on early in the morning about breakfast, rode all day on the railroad, and about dark reached a fort [Bridger?]. I stayed there two days, and then took a passenger train, and the next morning got to Fort Hall. I saw the agent here, and he told me I could stay at the agency, but the chief of the Bannocks who was there took me to his camp near by. The Bannocks told me they were glad to see a Cheyenne and that we ought to make a treaty with the Bannocks."

For ten days Porcupine visited and talked with the chief and leading men of this tribe on the subject of inter-tribal relations, and doubtless including the strange tidings out of Nevada and his projected visit there. When Porcupine's party left Fort Hall it had grown with a liberal addition of Bannocks and Shoshones.

"We took the railroad to a little town near by," said Porcupine, "and then took a narrow-gauge road. We went on this, riding all night at a very fast rate of speed, and came to a town on a big lake [Ogden or Salt Lake City]. We stayed there one day, taking the cars at night, rode all night, and next morning about 9 o'clock saw a settlement of Indians. We traveled south, going on a narrow-gauge road. We got off at this Indian town. The Indians here were different from any Indians I ever saw. The women and men were dressed in white people's clothes, the women having their hair banged. These Indians had their faces painted white, with black spots.

"We stayed with these people all day. We took the same road at night and kept on. We traveled all night, and about daylight we saw a lot of houses, and they told us there were a lot more Indians there; so we got off, and there is where we saw Indians living in huts of grass [probably tulé]. We stopped here and got something to eat. There were whites living near by. We got on the cars again at night, and during the night we got among some Indians, who were fish-eaters [Paiute]. We stayed among the Fish-eaters till morning, and then got into a wagon with the son of the chief of the Fish-eaters, and we arrived about noon at an agency on a big river. There was also a big lake near the agency.[17]

"From this agency we went back to the station, and they told us there were some more Indians to the south. One of the chiefs of the Fish-eaters then furnished us with four wagons. We traveled all day, and then came to another railroad. We left our wagons here and took the railroad, the Fish-eaters telling us there were some more Indians along the railroad who wanted to see us. We took this railroad about 2 o'clock and about sun down got to another agency, where there were more Fish-eaters."

From the statements of Porcupine and the rough diagrams and maps drawn by him for Major Carroll, there can be little doubt the involved trip had brought them into the land of the Paiutes, that they had visited

Pyramid and Walker lakes and their agencies, and that they were now in the vicinity of Mason Valley on the Walker River. Porcupine told of witnessing the dance through his travels. "All the Indians from the Bannock agency down to where I finally stopped danced this dance," he revealed, "the whites often dancing it themselves." He had traveled almost the whole distance across Mormon country.

"I will tell you about it," he said. "I want you all to listen to this, so that there will be no mistake. There is no harm in what I am going to say to anyone. . . . In the dance we had there [in Nevada] the whites and Indians danced together. I met there a great many kinds of people, but they all seemed to know about this religion. The people there seemed all to be good. I never saw any drinking or fighting or bad conduct among them. They treated me well on the cars, without pay. They gave me food without charge, and I found that this was a habit among them toward their neighbors. I thought it strange that the people there should have been so good, so different from those here.[18]

"What I am going to say is the truth. The two men sitting near me were with me, and will bear witness that I speak the truth. I and my people have been living in ignorance until I went and found out the truth. I never knew this before.

The Ghost Dance Goes East

"The Fish-eaters near Pyramid Lake told me that Christ had appeared on earth again. They said Christ knew he was coming, that eleven of his children were also coming from a far land. It appeared that Christ had sent for me to go there, and that was why unconsciously I took my journey. It had been foreordained. Christ had summoned myself and others from all heathen tribes, from two to three or four from each of fifteen or sixteen different tribes. There were more different languages than I ever heard before and I did not understand any of them. They told me when I got there that my great father was there also, but I did not know who he was.

"The people assembled, called a council, and the chief's son went to see the Great Father [Wovoka], who sent word for us to remain fourteen days in that camp, and that he would come to see us. He sent me a small package of something white to eat that I did not know the name of. There were a great many people in the council, and this white food was divided among them. The food was a big white nut. Then I went to the agency at Walker Lake and they told us Christ [Wovoka] would be there in two days. At the end of two days, on the third morning, hundreds of people gathered at this place. They cleared off a place near the agency in the form of a circus ring and we all gathered there. This space was perfectly cleared of grass, etc. We waited there till late in the evening, anxious to see Christ.

"Just before sundown I saw a great many people, mostly Indians, coming dressed in white men's clothes. The Christ was with them. They all formed in this ring around it. They put up sheets all around the circle, as they had no tents. Just after dark some of the Indians told me that the Christ was arrived. I looked around to see him, and finally saw him sitting on one side of the ring. They all started toward him, to see him. They made a big fire to throw light on him. I never looked around but went forward, and when I saw him, I bent my head. I had always thought the Great Father was a white man, but this man looked like an Indian. He sat there a long time and nobody went up to speak to him. He sat with his head bowed all the time.

"After awhile he rose, and said he was very glad to see his children. 'I have sent for you, and I am glad to see you. I am going to talk to you after awhile about your relatives who are dead and gone. My children, I want you to listen to all I have to say to you. I will teach you, too, how to dance a dance, and I want you to dance it. Get ready for your dance and then, when the dance is over, I will talk to you.'

"He was dressed in a white coat with stripes. The rest of his dress was a white man's except that he had on a pair of moccasins. Then he commenced our dance, everybody joining in, the Christ singing while we danced. We danced till late in the night, when he told us we had danced enough.

"The next morning, after breakfast was over, we went into the circle and spread canvas over it on the ground, the Christ standing in the midst of us. He told us he was going away that day, but would be back that next morning and talk to us.

"In the night when I first saw him I thought he was an Indian, but the next day when I could see better he looked different. He was not so dark as an Indian, nor so light as a white man. He had no beard or whiskers, but very heavy eyebrows. He was a good-looking man. We were crowded up very close. We had been told that nobody was to talk, and even if we whispered the Christ would know it. I had heard that Christ had been crucified, and I looked to see, and I saw a scar on his wrist and one on his face, and he seemed to be the man. I could not see his feet. He would talk to us all that day.

"That evening we all assembled to see him depart. When we were assembled, he began to sing, and he commenced to tremble all over, violently for a while,[19] and then sat down. We danced all that night, the Christ lying down beside us, apparently dead.

"The next morning when we went to eat breakfast, the Christ was with us. After breakfast four heralds went around and called out that the Christ was back with us, and wanted to talk to us. The circle was prepared again. The people assembled, and Christ came among us and sat down. He said he wanted to talk to us again, and for us to listen.

"He said: 'I am the man who made everything you see around you. I am not lying to you, my children. I made this earth and everything on it. I have been to heaven and seen your dead friends, and I have seen my own father and mother. In the beginning, after God made the earth, they sent me back to teach the people, and when I came back on earth the people were afraid of me and treated me badly. This is what they did to me [showing his scars]. I did not try to defend myself. I found my children were bad, so went back to heaven and left them. I told them that in so many hundred years I would come back to see my children. At the end of this time I was sent back to try to teach them. My father told me the earth was getting old and worn out, and the people getting bad, and that I was to renew everything as it used to be, and make it better.'

THE GHOST DANCE OF THE PLAINS TRIBES

Composite drawing by Mary Irvin Wright after a photograph by James Mooney.

—*Courtesy Bureau of American Ethnology.*

PINE RIDGE AGENCY, 1890

Photograph of Sioux gathering and dance about the time of Sitting Bull's assassination and the massacre at Wounded Knee.

—*From the Reynolds collection, courtesy of J. E. Reynolds.*

"He told us also that all our dead were to be resurrected; that they were all to come back to earth, and that as the earth was too small for them and us, he would do away with heaven, and make the earth itself large enough to contain us all; that we must tell all the people we meet about these things.

"He spoke to us about fighting, and said that was bad, and we must keep from it; that the earth was to be all good hereafter, and we must all be friends with one another. He said that in the fall of the year the youth of all the good people would be renewed, so that nobody would be more than 40 years old, and that if they behaved themselves well after this the youth of everyone would be renewed in the spring. He said if we were all good he would send people among us who could heal all our wounds and sickness by mere touch, and that we would live forever.

"He told us not to quarrel, or fight, nor strike each other, nor shoot one another; that the whites and Indians were to be all one people. He said if any man disobeyed what he ordered, his tribe would be wiped from the face of the earth; that we must believe everything he said, and that we must not doubt him, or say he lied; that if we did, he would know it; that he would know our thoughts and actions, in no matter what part of the world we might be. . . .

"Ever since the Christ I speak of talked to me I have thought what he said was good. I see nothing bad in it. When we got back, I knew my people were bad, and had heard nothing of all this, so I got them together and told them of it, and warned them to listen to it for their own good. I talked to them for four nights and five days. I told them just what I have told you here today. I told them what I said were the words of God Almighty, who was looking down on them. ...

"If any one of you think I am not telling the truth, you can go and see this man I speak of for yourselves. I will go with you, and I would like one or two of my people who doubt me to go with me.

"The Christ talked to us all in our respective tongues. You can see this man in your sleep any time you want after you have seen him and shaken hands with him once. Through him you can go to heaven and meet your friends ..."[20]

The report of this delegation to their people as voiced by Porcupine, caused wild excitement, and set the Cheyennes, and the Sioux to dancing in the pattern already intimately known to the Bannocks and the Shoshones. A council of the Cheyennes was called to hear Porcupine and, as mentioned in his own statement, he talked to his people five days in succession regarding the Nevada Messiah and his doctrine. By

June of 1890 the dance had become so prevalent among the Cheyennes that American authorities became alarmed, took steps to suppress it, and in the hurried investigation of the craze now generally epidemic across America, wrung from the enlightened Porcupine this amazing and revealing story of his journey, and the statement of the faith already ringing joyously in the hearts of thousands upon thousands of Indians.

Short Bull carried the message to the Oglala Sioux simultaneously with Porcupine's conversion of his people. He found little resistance to the doctrine, for already the Shoshoni and the Arapahoe had passed on to the tribe, in substance, most of the information he himself had obtained from the Messiah. Immediately another delegation, headed by Good Thunder, traveled west to Nevada in search of greater enlightenment. "On their return they announced that the Messiah had indeed come to help the Indians, but not the whites. Their report aroused a fervor of joyful excitement among the Indians and a second delegation was sent out in 1890, consisting of Good Thunder, Cloud Horse, Yellow Knife, and Short Bull. They confirmed the report of the first delegation, and on this assurance the Ghost Dance was inaugurated among the Sioux at Pine Ridge in the spring of 1890."[21]

George Sword, formerly captain of the Indian police at Pine Ridge agency, and at that time serving as judge of the Indian court, meticulously wrote down in the Teton Dakota dialect, the report of these journeying delegations in search of truth. Translated by an Indian for Miss Emma C. Sickels,[22] it became a part of the documentary files of this strange religious movement in the Bureau of Ethnology, at Washington:

". . . The Oglala heard that the Son of God was truly on earth in the west from their country. This was in the year 1889. The first people knew about the messiah to be on earth were the Shoshoni and Arapahoe. So in 1889 Good Thunder with four or five others visited the place where Son of God said to be . . . They said the messiah was there at the place, but he was there to help the Indians and not the whites; so this made the Indians happy to find out this. Good Thunder, Cloud Horse, Yellow Knife, and Short Bull visited the place again in 1890 and saw the messiah. Their story of visit to the messiah is as follows:

" 'From the country where the Arapaho and Shoshoni we start in the direction of northwest in train for five nights and arrived at the foot of the Rocky mountains. Here we saw him and also several other tribes of Indians. The people said that the messiah will come at a place in the woods where the place was prepare for him. When we went to the place a smoke descended from heaven to the place where he was to come. When the smoke disappeared, there was a man of about forty, which was the Son of God. The man said:

" ' "My grandchildren! I am glad you have come far away to see your relatives. This are your people who have come back from your country." When he said he want us to go with him, we looked and we saw a land created across the ocean on which all the nations of Indians were coming home, but, as the messiah looked at the land which was created and reached across the ocean, again disappeared, saying that it was not time for that to take place. The messiah then gave to Good Thunder some paints—Indian paint and a white paint —a green grass [sagebrush twigs?]; and said, "My grandchildren, when you get home, go to farming and send all your children to school. And on way home if you kill any buffalo cut the head, the tail, and the four feet and leave them, and that buffalo will come to live again. When the soldiers of the white people chief want to arrest me, I shall stretch out my arms, which will knock them to nothingness, or, if not that, the earth will open and swallow them in. My Father commanded me to visit the Indians on a purpose. I have came to the white people first, but they not good. They killed me, and you can see the marks of my wounds on my feet, my hands, and on my back . . . I want you to tell when you get home your people to follow my examples. Any one Indian does not obey me and tries to be on white's side will be covered over by a new land that is to come over this old one. You will, all the people, use the paints and grass I give you. In the spring when the green grass comes, your people who have gone before you will come back, and you shall see your friends then, for you have come to my call."

" 'The people from every tipi send for us to visit them. They are people who died many years ago. Chasing Hawk, who died not long ago, was there, and we went to his tipi. He was living with his wife, who was killed in war long ago . . . A son of Good Thunder who died in war long ago was one who also took us to his tipi, so his father saw him. When coming we come to a herd of buffaloes. We killed one and took everything except the four feet, head, and tail, and when we came a little ways from it, there was the buffaloes come to life again and went off. This was one of the messiah's word came to truth. The messiah said, "I will short your journey when you feel tired of the long ways, if you call upon me." This we did when we were tired. The night came upon us, we stopped at a place, and we called upon the messiah to help us, because we were tired of long journey. We went to sleep, and in the morning we found ourselves at a great distance from where we stopped.' ..."[23]

The new religion, along with its Messiah, now had its miracles. It now had its traveling Pauls, Peters, and a multiplying array of witnesses who added to the wonders they had seen with every mile they journeyed eastward. In the Carlisle-trained students of the various tribes, who had learned to write the white man's language, it had its recorders and letter writers, who passed the tidings along from tribe to tribe, and who already were settling its form into a body of written testament. The Messiah had made his appearance upon the earth. Wonder of wonders, he was an Indian, spoke as an Indian, and instead of diverting his attention to the hated whites, was interested solely in making a new and happier world for Indians alone. Ten thousand Indians listened to the new voice, and clung with bated eagerness on every word that came out of the west.

X

BULLET-PROOF

I am the man who made everything you see around you . . . I made the earth and everything on it. I have been to heaven and seen your dear dead friends and have seen my own father and mother. —WOVOKA.

IN THE years preceding Wovoka's translation and his emergence as Christ and Savior to the Indian world, the Mormons from Salt Lake City and their outlying towns in Utah and Nevada, had made their great strides in conversion of the Paiute nation to the doctrines and practices of their church. Their peculiar teachings regarding the Israelitish background of the American Indian, the *Book of the Mormon* with its purported history of this fallen people, its promise of their redemption and rise again to greatness, its story of Christ's ministry among them, and His promise to return,[24] had been assimilated and accepted by hundreds upon hundreds of Paiutes, long before Wovoka stepped into the center of the spiritual stage. While intrigued by Mormon doctrine, there is no indication that he ever personally entered the waters of Mormon bap-

tism. His was not the nature to serve as humble convert, yearning over the promises of a savior's return
and ephemeral predictions of the Indian millennium.
He *was* their savior, and the millennium was here
and now. But he did find that Mormons had conveniently prepared the way. He found his easiest and most
enthusiastic converts among those who already had
embraced the tenets of that faith.

The first temple completed in the west by the Mormons was at St. George, on the Virgin River, in southern
Utah. At that time there were far more Paiutes in
this vicinity than there were Mormons. Jacob Hamblin[25] and other great Mormon Indian missionaries had
converted almost to a man the tribes and clans of
Paiutes in southern Utah and eastern Nevada, and
many of the first to enter the great white sanctuary
at St. George, to receive the higher "endowments"
and deeper mysteries of the faith, were Indians. With
these initiations came the privilege of henceforth wearing the holy undergarment, which acknowledged its
wearer to the privilege of the celestial glory after death,
and whose sacred markings were a protection against
physical harm and satanic influences. Those Indians
who had taken these higher Mormon vows were, like
their white counterparts, elders in the church, and

bearers of its Melchizedek priesthood. Among the Paiutes there were many of them.[26]

In the shuffling circles of the ghost dance throughout
the Paiute nation were many of these Paiute Mormon
elders. They talked to Wovoka, and he was cognizant
of the holy garment they wore, and which was accepted
by them as an actual physical protection against disease and death. Their secrecy about the especial mean-
ings of the "marks" upon them, whose potent magic
made an ordinary undergarment into a shield of protection, irked Wovoka. Their explanation that one must
enter the Temple of the Lord in order to be privileged,
initiated and chosen, was an angle of meaning which
the Indian Savior did not too closely pursue. To his
people, and to himself, he *was* the Temple of the Lord.
And his Mormon initiates, in accepting him as "Our
Father," hardly considered it in the realm of necessity
for him to make the pilgrimage to St. George.

The one claim Wovoka never ceased to stress in his
talks and demonstrations before the pilgrims of the
many tribes who visited him, was the fact that he was
inviolate. Those who had traveled so far to stand in awe
before him, were under the natural assumption that as
the Messiah, he was immune from death; that the bullets of the enemy had no effect upon him; that he had
long since been lifted from the menaces of disease and

pain. The physical marks of the cross were easily cut or tattooed into the hands and feet, but the triumph over death and disease was something he daily reiterated, with the knowledge in his heart that he was preaching from a shaky premise. It hurt just as much to cut a wound in the palm of his hand as it did in the nailings to the cross in the dim past of history. He had all but died from scarlet fever, and in his heart he was still as frightened of measles, syphilis and smallpox as he ever had been. But those who came a thousand miles to sit in wonder at his feet not only expected "Our Father" to be inviolate, but capable of rising into heaven, or dwelling in the earthly body at will.

Still there were skeptics, who demanded proof that bullets of the soldiers would not kill him, as they had killed so many thousands of Indians before him. Occasionally there would be one who would suggest that if he were indeed the Messiah, and inviolate, that he stand up, and allow someone to shoot at him. And there was always the danger that someone might someday try it. Fortunately, most everyone who visited him went away convinced. Dissenters were howled down by the chants of the faithful. The wonderful visits to heaven made by the dancers who fell prostrate to the ground, were convincing enough without the Messiah having to make a human target of himself to prove that he had conquered death.

Yet there were always the whispers of a man's conscience, and the challenge of necessity. Except for the fact that he must suffer and die like other men, he was almost convinced he *was* the Christ. When he stood before his people, when he danced with them in the line, when he dropped to the earth in catalepsis, and his soul was borne aloft, he *knew* he was the Christ, just as certainly as those around him knew it. But after the frenzy was over, and his people had departed, came again the doubts. Only the question of inviolability stood in the way of conviction. In the face of this question, he still had to cover, and he still had to lie. Often did he wish that he might have something similar to a Mormon garment that would convincingly protect him, that would magically turn back both pain and bullets. He knew he was an adept at using trickery in such things, but in the high plane of his great mission he had found it unnecessary now to resort to fakery. Still always there were those skeptics. Maybe one dramatic demonstration of inviolability would silence both the dissenters and his conscience. To conquer, one must sometimes stoop.

Many times, on rabbit drives, Wovoka had mystified his fellow tribesmen with a simple trick from his repertoire of legerdemain. Deliberately and carefully he would call attention to the fact he had no need of conventional powder and shot—by simply dropping into the muzzle of his gun a pinch of sand or snow, ramming it home, and then knocking over his rabbit with the blast. The gullible Paiutes seemed never to see the necessity of questioning the fact that a normal load of powder and shot lay behind whatever their prophet may have tamped into his gun barrel.[27]

For his miracle this time the stage was as carefully set as it had been on the day he brought ice down the Walker River. On the chosen night, before three hundred assembled Indians, including emissaries from such nations as the Sioux and the Cheyenne, he stripped to the waist, slipped on a shirt upon which, with the magic red ochre he had painted various protective symbols. Then he handed a loaded shotgun to one of his disciples. Standing in the middle of a blanket, and while the night fire played mystic patterns around the hushed and silent multitude, he stood like a crossed-armed god while the other Indian lowered the shotgun, at ten paces, and aimed at his chest.

Not a whisper disturbed the drama of the moment. Hiss and crackle of the fire, the heavy breathing of the spectators, and the metallic chitter of crickets in the brush outside the margins of the hard-packed arena, were sound and background to the picture, as the stocky frame of Our Father, in its weird shirt, waited stoically for the blast to come. Nervously the disciple squeezed both triggers of the double-barreled gun. A blast of flame shot out, and the gun roared. The spectators saw Wovoka bend, as though with the impact of the charge. Buckshot spilled generously over the blanket, and in the clearing smoke, it was plain that Wovoka still lived.

There was no blood. The buckshot, conveniently spewed from his hand at the precise moment, lay at his feet. The shirt had not a single hole in it. As a demonstration of inviolability, it was convincing.

Eager hands grabbed up the buckshot that so mysteriously had been repelled by the shirt. Each single pellet, like anything that had ever touched the Messiah, would be treasured as the most sacred sort of medicine by anyone lucky enough to find one. Even the empty cartridges, ejected from the gun, became mystic emblems to be borne away from Mason Valley as testimony to the new religion. The paper waddings, which Wovoka had substituted for actual buckshot in the loads, had been too certainly blown to bits to be picked up, otherwise they would have been appropriated by the eager throng. But it was the shirt which became the prize of all—the magic garment which turned away bullets. Gravely, deliberately, Our Father took it off, carried it to a spot where he had tied a rope between two low trees. Carefully he pinned the shirt to the line, so it hung limply in the air. He then invited anyone present to shoot at it. A moment later several guns roared. He then took down the shirt, and allowed those present to examine it. That there were no holes in it could be explained by the fact that a bullet propelled by a black powder charge would waft the flimsy shirt aside without penetration. But those assembled were convinced they had witnessed a twin miracle.

Which man got the magic shirt, or to what tribe it went, no man knows for certainty. But had Wovoka turned his prophetic eyes toward the monstrous thing that was to come of it, he would gladly have wished for the death which he had gone to such pains to prove as impossible.

TYPICAL GHOST SHIRT OF THE PLAINS TRIBES

—*Courtesy Bureau of American Ethnology.*

SITTING BULL, THE GREAT SIOUX CHIEF
Shot by American troops because of his activities in and promotion of the
Ghost Dance. Photograph by D. F. Barry, 1885.

—*Courtesy Bureau of American Ethnology.*

XI

Sitting Bull and the Sioux

God Almighty did not make me an agency Indian, and I'll fight and die fighting before any white man can make me an agency Indian. —SITTING BULL.

THE TRAGIC fall and final humiliation of the Sioux nation at the hands of the white man is enough to make any honorable American writhe in shame. Known in their own tongue as the *La-ko-tas* (which the first white men quickly transformed into Dakotas), they were a numerous, proud and warlike race whose homelands, north of the Arkansas, stretched from the Mississippi to the Rocky Mountains. Living in a great and favored land of plenty, where buffalo and game covered the face of the earth in lavish abundance, they were, as Indians measured wealth, both rich and fortunate. As tamers and users of the horse, their men of magnificent physique and limitless courage, they not only were the true aristocrats of North America, but probably the greatest cavalrymen the world has ever known.

Their tribe was subdivided into seven great families, known as (1) the *Si-cangu, Brule,* or Burnt Thighs; (2) the *I-ttaz-ip-co, Sans Arcs,* or No Bows; (3) the *Si-ha-sa-pa,* or Blackfoot; (4) the *Mi-ni-kan-ye,* or Those Who Plant by the Water; (5) the *Oo-hen-on-pa,* or Two Kettles; (6) the *O-gal-lal-las,* or Wanderers in the Mountains; and (7) the *Unk-pa-pas,* or Those Who Dwell by Themselves. It was to the last clan, the Unk-pa-pa, Teton Sioux, that Sitting Bull, the great chief and statesman, belonged.[28]

George Catlin, artist, writer, and one of their early visitors, spoke of the Sioux Nation: "This tribe is one of the most numerous in North America, and also one of the most vigorous and warlike tribes to be found, numbering some forty or fifty thousand, and able undoubtedly to muster, if the tribe could be moved simultaneously, at least eight or ten thousand warriors, well mounted and well armed. This tribe takes vast numbers of the wild horses on the plains toward the Rocky Mountains, and many of them have been supplied with guns; but the greater part of them hunt with their bows and arrows and long lances, killing their game from their horses' backs while at full speed.

". . . The personal appearance of these people is very fine and prepossessing, their persons tall and straight, and their movements elastic and graceful . . . furnishing at least one-half of their warriors of six feet or more in height . . .

"The family of Sioux, who occupy so vast a tract of country, extending from the banks of the Mississippi River to the base of the Rocky Mountains, are everywhere a migratory or roaming tribe, divided into forty-two bands or families, each having a chief, who all acknowledge a superior or head chief, to whom they all are held subordinate . . .

"There is no tribe on the continent, perhaps, of finer looking men than the Sioux; and few tribes who are better or more comfortably clad, and supplied with the necessaries of life. There are no parts of the great plains of America which are more abundantly stocked with buffaloes and wild horses, nor any people more bold in destroying the one for food, and appropriating the other to their use."

In answer to the then current belief that the American Indian was a "poor, drunken, murderous wretch," Catlin observed of the Sioux: "I have traveled several years already amongst these people and I have not had my scalp taken, nor a blow struck at me; nor had occasion to raise my hand against an Indian; nor has my property been stolen as yet, to my knowledge, to the value of a shilling; and that in a country where no man is punishable by law for the crime of stealing . . . That the Indians in their native state are drunken, is false; for they are the only temperance people, literally speaking, that ever I saw in my travels, or ever expect to see . . . for these people manufacture no spirituous liquors themselves, and know nothing of it until it is brought into their country and tendered to them by Christians. That these people are naked is equally untrue, and is easily disproved; for I am sure that with the paintings I have made . . . and with their beautiful costumes, which I have procured and shall bring home, I shall be able to establish the fact that many of these people dress, not only with clothes comfortable for any latitude, but that they also dress with some considerable taste and elegance. Nor am I quite sure that they are entitled to the name of poor, who live in a boundless country of green fields, with good horses to ride; where they are all joint tenants of the soil together; where the Great Spirit has supplied them with an abundance of food to eat—where they are all indulging in the pleasures and amusements of a lifetime of idleness and ease, with no business hours to attend to, or professions to learn—where there are no notes in bank or other debts to pay—no taxes, no tithes, no rents, nor beggars to touch and tax the sympathy of their souls at every step they go."[29]

But Catlin saw the Sioux in their golden age—before the white man had decimated the buffalo, before white miners and white cattle barons had stolen their birthright and ejected them from the lands of their fathers.

The buffalo meant food, warmth and housing to Indians of the American plains. Bison were hunted and killed only for their immediate needs—not for love of slaughter, and not for profit. When organized white hunters began stalking the animal for its leather, and for the sheer joy of seeing how many of the huge, lumbering beasts could be dispatched in a single day, a dark and melancholy era was ushered in for such nations as the Comanches, Cheyennes, and the Sioux. The Sioux in particular resisted the encroachment of the white man upon his vital lands and food supply. The uprisings of the Sioux under Red Cloud and Sitting Bull, from the massacres of 1862 and the annihilation of Custer and his army, down to the final, sordid bloodbath at Wounded Knee, were no more than a proud nation battling for its right to exist.

Sitting Bull, the great chief of the Sioux, became a living symbol of this resistance. So long as he lived, no matter how pitifully reduced, or how hungry they were as a people, there was hope; for Sitting Bull was an implacable foe of the insidious outrages perpetrated by the white man against his people. With his assassination, because he espoused the doctrine of Wovoka and the ghost dance as the last tiny hope of redemption and return for the Sioux as a people, the light finally went out for this valiant nation.

Sitting Bull was born at a camp on Grand River, not far from the present town of Bullhead, South Dakota, somewhere near 1830. He was born into royal parentage, the son of Jumping Bull, a Sioux chief, and a nephew of Four Horns and Hunting His Lodge, who likewise were chiefs. For an Indian, his father was wealthy, an owner of many fast horses, "in four colors."

"Sitting Bull, who at first was called Sacred Standshot, soon became a famous hunter. At ten years old he was famous all through the tribe as a killer of buffalo calves. As his father was rich and did not need the meat, the boy gave away all the game he killed to the poorer members of the tribe, and thus gained great popularity . . ."

At the age of fourteen the precocious youth had met a man in mortal combat, and had succeeded in killing his adversary.

"Before he reached his fifteenth year Sitting Bull began to develop those traits which afterward made him a terror to the white settlers of the frontier. He is described by an old Western scout as a boy of rather

stocky appearance, not 'straight as an arrow' like the
traditional Indian, and not given to any of those boyish
sports which Fenimore Cooper has set as a standard.

"He was lazy and vicious . . . but with all these traits
he was fearless under all circumstances, a magnificent
rider, an accurate shot, and capable of enduring an
extraordinary amount of fatigue. As he approached 21
the cruelty became more marked, but he did nothing to
indicate that he had in him the making of one of the
representative men of his race."[30]

In single-handed combat with a Crow chief, in
which the fearless young man's gun and knife sped the
chief on to the happy hunting ground, Sitting Bull
received a bullet which, at close range, tore into his
left foot and left him with the crippling limp which
remained throughout his life. It is generally believed
that this limp was genesis of the name by which the
Hunkpapa knew him—Lame Bull, or Sitting Bull. Stanley Vestal, as biographer to the man, takes vigorous
and scholarly exception not only to this statement, but
also to the popular belief that the great Sioux leader
was not a war chief, but only a medicine man. The
name Sitting Bull, according to Vestal, was bestowed
upon the young warrior by Returns-Again, a Sioux
mystic who had heard the name muttered by a mighty
buffalo bull—the sacred animal—prototype of the

Sioux god who was "patron of both sexes, of generosity, fecundity, industry, and ceremonies." And because all hunters revered the Buffalo God, because he controlled the fortunes of the hunt, and because a great buffalo bull had actually spoken the name, Returns-Again bestowed it upon the most worthy and bravest of the Hunkpapa young men. Sitting Bull was verily named by the gods themselves.

"He was three times married, one of his wives dying soon after the wedding. The other two wives were named She That Was Seen by the Nation, and She Had Four Robes. They bore in all nine children, including a pair of twins—a most unusual thing among Indians. When, after the Custer massacre, Sitting Bull at last surrendered at Fort Buford, one of his sons, a young man of 18, was at school in Chicago. Another, a boy of six years, was with the chief, and at the formal powwow the chief put his heavy rifle in the little fellow's hands and ordered him to give it to Major Brotherton, saying: 'I surrender this rifle to you through my young son, whom I now desire to teach in this way that he has become a friend of the whites. I wish him to live as the whites do and be taught in their schools. I wish to be remembered as the last man of my tribe who gave up his rifle. This boy has now given it to you, and he wants to know how he is going to make a living.' "[32]

Sitting Bull was both warrior and deeply religious mystic. By birth and prowess he held chieftainship of a part of the Sioux tribe, but "his remarkable ascendancy over the whole tribe or nation was due to his miracle-working and to his talents as a politician. He played upon the credulity of the Sioux with his 'medicine' or pretended miracles, until they believed him to possess supernatural powers, and they were ready to follow his lead in everything. Some other chiefs inherited wider authority, such as Red Cloud and Crazy Horse, and some minor chiefs were inclined now and then to dispute his sway, such as Gall, Rain-in-the-face, and Broad Tail. But when Sitting Bull made an appeal to the religious fanaticism of the people, there was no withstanding him. To the day of his death he was the principal chief of all the Sioux and leader of 6,000 braves, who at all times were ready at his command to commit any crime from murder up or down."[33]

Sitting Bull's relentless battle against the encroaching white man opened with forays and scalping raids on wagon trains and settlers. But in 1866, with his vicious raid on Fort Buford, he became widely known to the American people as an enemy who gave no quarter, and asked none. His reputation for savagery was such that, at this incident, the commandant of Fort Buford shot and killed his own wife rather than allow her to fall into the hands of the Sioux.

In attitude he was marked by a consuming hatred for the whites, and toward them. Unless boxed into a corner, he was impudent and defiant. Actually he spoke a little English, and had a conversing knowledge of French, due to his sojourn with the Red River half-breeds in Canada, but after his ascendancy to chieftainship, and because of his contempt for the white man, he would never converse in the white man's language, admit that he understood it, or allow it to be spoken in his presence. "This hatred for the whites distinguished Sitting Bull above all other Sioux. When he was engaged in hostilities he was as ferocious and bloodthirsty as a beast of prey . . . In peace he was a smooth liar, and, professing the utmost friendship, never failed to be insolent and insulting when the opportunity offered."[34]

For ten years, by bloody engagements and desultory peace conferences, Sitting Bull made his presence and his pressure felt upon the American people in their expansion as a nation. Only the bravest dared settle in the Sioux country, and an alert army was a constant necessity to cope with the bloody ingenuity and superb generalship of the wily chief. But the zenith of Sitting

Bull's fame and power was reached in the Sioux War of 1876.

Source of this tragic conflict was the discovery of gold and silver in the Black Hills, part of the Sioux domain set aside by Congressional and Presidential order. When it became generally known that precious metals were to be found in this little-known region, the heaviest pressure was brought to bear upon the government for the region's opening to prospectors and miners. A "military reconnaissance" expedition of twelve hundred men and sixty Indian guides was fitted out. It was led by General George A. Custer. Actually, it was a well-equipped prospecting party, on the grand scale. The expedition's report from the Black Hills was that the region was rich with precious metals. A stampede of miners and settlers inevitably followed.

Red Cloud, Spotted Tail, and other chiefs visited Washington in protest of this blatant violation of existing treaties. They succeeded in getting a promise from the government that Americans would be kept out of the area. But, like nearly every other Indian agreement out of Washington, the promise was never kept. By 1875 a thousand miners were at work in the Black Hills.

Next the Sioux demanded payment for the lands of which they were being robbed. A governmental commission visited them, to agree on terms. No terms were reached, and nothing beneficial came out of it. The Sioux, at last convinced that they would have to fight for their rights, commenced deserting the conservative leadership of Red Cloud and Spotted Tail, and flocked to Sitting Bull, who never ceased to be truculent about the invasion, and opposed the selling of Sioux acreage at any price.

Those of the Sioux opposed to war, but knowing now that a full scale war was imminent, fled to the agencies at Standing Rock, Spotted Tail, and Cheyenne River. However, this still left Sitting Bull with a formidable force of 3,500 mounted warriors, spoiling for a fight. The American Army, under General George Crook, was ordered to move against those hostile Sioux, and at the same time an order was issued demanding that Sitting Bull and those chiefs operating with him, report at their reservations before January 1, 1876, otherwise the United States would make war against them.

Sitting Bull and his men impudently ignored the ultimatum, and in January the first engagements with the United States troops occurred, with negligible loss to the Indians. Sitting Bull and his hostiles set up their camps on the Big Horn and Tongue Rivers, in the Valley of the Yellowstone. The government dispatched scouts into the Big Horn country with a peremptory notice of ejection, and the heavy promise that if the recalcitrant chief and his warriors did not heed the summons, troops would be sent to drive them out. Sitting Bull received the notice with contempt. "When you come for me, you need bring no guides," he said. "You will easily find me. I shall be right here. I shall not run away."

All available troops were ordered into action. Three columns, under command of Generals Gibbon, Terry and Crook, moved toward Sitting Bull's camp in the Big Horn country. These three columns were to meet on the Powder or Tongue River, and combine forces in the heart of the enemy's hideout. The plan was for General Crook to move from Fort Reno northward; General Terry, with General Custer's cavalry, from Fort Lincoln, was to march west; and General Gibbon, from Fort Buford, was to descend the Yellowstone Valley, there to join with Terry's men.

Terry's army, with the 7th Cavalry, in total numbering a thousand men, set out May 7. By May 29 they had reached the Little Missouri. Terry's main column reached the Yellowstone June 11, and went into camp. General Gibbon's forces had arrived at a point on the opposite bank, not more than thirty-five miles away. General Crook and his forces had not yet made contact.

Strategy while awaiting the juncture of Crook's command was for Gibbon's forces to move to the mouth of the Rosebud River, to prevent the escape of Sitting Bull's hostiles across that stream. Terry's force was to ascend the Yellowstone as far as the Tongue River, and there await the return of a scouting party under Colonel Reno. General Custer was to take nine companies of cavalry, a detachment of Indian scouts, and a large train of mules loaded with supplies enough for fifteen days, push up the valley of the Tongue, and then strike out on forced march across country to the Rosebud River, where the Sioux were reported to be in strong force. There they were to rejoin the main column at the mouth of the river.

What happened to Custer and his magnificent little army at the hands of Sitting Bull and his Sioux, has been told and retold a thousand times. General Crook was being forced to fight his way northward against determined resistance of the Sioux, but in spite of harassment and losses, he was managing to keep his forces intact. But of Custer and his men, none lived to tell the story of their tragic battle with the Sioux. In the Valley of the Little Big Horn, they had been surprised by Sitting Bull's forces, surrounded, and slaughtered to a man. Custer's fellow troopers arrived far too late to effect a rescue. All they found was a valley silent with the hideous remains of carnage and death.

Sitting Bull and the Sioux

The American army never prevailed over Sitting Bull and his hostile Sioux. Instead of returning the defiant Indians to their reservations, instead of avenging the ghastly defeat of Custer, the joint expedition was forced to return empty-handed. The Bull and his men vanished as ubiquitiously as they had appeared. Not until later was it learned that the fighting Sioux had crossed the border into Canada, and had there found sanctuary at Fort Walsh, in the British Northwest Territory.

In October of 1876 a commission, headed by General Terry, went to Canada in an effort to woo Sitting Bull and his warriors back to the United States and their respective reservations. The commission was cordially and politely received by the Dominion authorities, and a pow-wow arranged with the rebellious chieftain. Results can best be summed up by the report of a news correspondent who accompanied the mission northward:

"The United States Commission sent out by the Government to find and treat for peace and good will with the Sioux chief Sitting Bull, has at length succeeded in coming face to face with the redoubtable Indian chieftain and have failed to bring him to any terms. In short, the commission has met Sitting Bull and Sitting Bull has dismissed it abruptly and disdainfully. The expedition has failed in its purpose and the Sioux question is as far from a satisfactory solution as when Gen. Terry and his brother commissioners first set out on their long and tedious journey to the Northwest."[35]

At General Terry's suggestion that amnesty would be granted, that Sitting Bull and his band return and settle at the agency, and that they surrender their horses and their arms, which would be sold and the money invested in cattle for them, Sitting Bull sneeringly replied: "For sixty-four years you have kept me and my people and treated us bad. What have *we* done that you should want us to stop? We have done nothing. It is all the people on your side that have started us to do all these depredations. We could not go anywhere else, and so we took refuge in this country. . .

"You see me? Here I am! If you think I am a fool, you are a bigger fool than I am . . . You came here to tell us lies, but we don't want to hear them . . . Don't you say two more words. Go back home, where you came from. This country is mine, and I intend to stay here. . ."[36]

XII

LAST OF A GREAT CHIEF

Let it be recorded that I was the last man of my people to lay down the gun.
—SITTING BULL.

THE Canadian exile of Sitting Bull lasted nearly four years, but to him as chief and leader of all the Sioux, it proved ruinous. To the Bull and his band, the British Government extended sanctuary, and that was all. They were given no supplies, or food; and raids, either in Canada or across the United States border, were forbidden, on pain of retribution or deportation. The comparatively barren land around Fort Walsh held no comparison to their once lush homelands of the Rosebud. Game was scarce, there was no buffalo, and forced to their own resources, the once proud and haughty band of warriors were soon in a state of starvation. During these years of exile they suffered indescribably from lack of food and clothing. Their women and children died from want, exposure and cold, and the braves vainly hunted for enough game to keep bodies and souls together.

Meanwhile Dakota was rapidly becoming civilized. The endless struggle to keep out the white man had utterly failed. The buffalo and antelope were fast disappearing from the ancestral hunting ground of the Sioux. "Sitting Bull kept himself fully posted as to the situation, and satisfied himself that he and his followers could not return except as prisoners. The chief could not keep this information to himself, and as a consequence dissatisfaction became widespread. He lost his power of keeping his followers together, and subchiefs led hundreds of the savages away in raiding bands; some of them came over the line and others hovered near the boundary."[37]

With the desertion of chiefs Gall and Crow King and the loss of their followers, the cause of Sitting Bull received its greatest hurt and humiliation. Returning to the United States, they surrendered to the authorities, and were placed upon the reservation, where they assumed posts of power and influence while their greater leader haughtily sulked out his time in Canada.

"Sitting Bull, however, stubbornly held out, hoping that the Canadian authorities would make terms for him with the Government at Washington. In this he was disappointed, and at last he found himself deserted by all but a few dozen of his old followers. Then a great blow fell upon him, which for the first time bowed his lofty spirit. A messenger brought him word that his favorite daughter Minnestema (Sleeping Water), a name conferred upon her by the whites, had run away with an Indian buck, who had subsequently abandoned her. These tidings well nigh broke Sitting Bull's heart. With all his faults he was an affectionate father, as most Indians are. Minnestema, the flower of his tribe, was his idol, and his pride was stung to the quick because the Indian who had so shamelessly deserted her was a man whom he despised. Humbled, despondent, broken in spirit, Sitting Bull decided to surrender."[38]

Sitting Bull returned to his people as shorn of power as though he never existed. He found them, even including his once mighty warriors of the Big Horn, abject reservation Indians. Arriving at Standing Rock Agency, protected by the guns of Fort Yates, he found his bitterest rival, Gall, in complete control of those Sioux who once had so loyally followed him. To see his lands filling up with the despised white men, to see his people at last subjugated to the American military, and the cause for which he stood forever lost, made this hour a bitter one.

In vain he now lifted his voice in the tribal oratory that once had held so persuasive an influence, and of which he was so adept. His people walked away and would not listen. As spiritual shaman, he sang the songs of once-known glory, and the warning songs which the spirits whispered into his soul. They ridiculed his prayers and incantations; they turned deaf ears to his chants. Their hearts were now for the favors and food of the Indian agents, who hated and feared this proud and unbending chieftain. The new crop of Sioux leaders, raised up in his absence by the reservation officials to serve their own needs, were just as anxious to be rid of this articulate voice of their own conscience. Sitting Bull's enemies were now in the saddle, and they hungered for his blood.

Finally, to put an end to his desperate intrigues, and fearing the ferment he again was attempting to agitate would put them in bad with United States authorities, the Sioux chiefs reported Sitting Bull to the military as again a dangerous character. To strip him forever of his power, and to humiliate him in the eyes of his people, the government ordered that Four Horns, uncle of the Bull, and now a decrepit, imbecilic old man, should rule the camp in place of his nephew. Sitting Bull, his two wives, and one hundred and forty-eight of his people were taken aboard a steamboat, and delivered to Fort Randall as prisoners of war.

To be detained as a common prisoner was more than the haughty chieftain could stand, and he wrote an abject letter to the United States Government begging them to allow him to return to the Grand River, the place of his birth. If they would allow him this last request, the chastened and defeated Bull promised he would henceforth wear the white man's clothes, and do all in his power to persuade the other men of his nation to do likewise. He had decided, he said, that there could be no more fighting on the part of his people, and that the next generation of Sioux would have to become mechanics and tillers of the soil, like their white conquerors.

At first the chary authorities allowed him only to return to Standing Rock Agency, but at last convinced of his sincerity, he was allowed to go to the valley of the Grand River to finish out his life in peaceful seclusion. Here, in the traditional sacred hunting grounds of the Sioux, and the richest area of their once immense tribal possessions, he built himself a log house on the river, and moved in with his wives and children.

Shorn now of his power, and displaced in leadership by the younger bloods who were coming to strength in the tribe, he lived here in comparative seclusion. And it was in this house that his enemies finally murdered him. Here he contemplated the tragedy that had struck the Indian nations of America, here he recounted the coups of his warrior days, here he carried on the more lonely rites of his "medicine."

At the urging of white men who had come to respect and champion the old battler, he was finally induced, in 1884, to make a tour of the white men's cities. He was placed on exhibit at such places as Y.M.C.A. Hall in Philadelphia, and white men paid their silver to see the man who had annihilated Custer. He visited Washington, and all the great cities of the east, and he made a tour with Buffalo Bill's Wild West Show, where he was accepted by the public as the show's star attraction. European tours were offered him, and honors and adulation were heaped upon him. But quickly wearying of his role as public curiosity, he returned to his little log hut on the Grand. The one gift that went with him, and of which he prized the most, was a trained gray circus horse, tendered him by his friend Buffalo Bill Cody.

The Sioux, including Sitting Bull and his most recalcitrant warriors, were now finally and completely wards of the government, and reservation Indians. In common with all the other American tribes forced into this unwanted and humiliating pattern, they were now at the mercy of the grafters, politicians, and dishonest officials who grew fat in their corruption while the Indian starved, or lived in almost constant want. Stripped of his power, the old chief could only brood over this tragic fate of a once proud and warlike nation, and look out in anger and sadness at the empty promises and broken faith that had come to them from the Great White Father at Washington.

"The year of 1890 was a hard one for the Indians. In addition to the broken faith of the Government, the swindling practices of its agents, and the unscrupulous aggressions of the settlers, they had to bear the burden of bad weather, poor crops, and a scarcity of game. Their complaints were just, and loud, and bitter; but were little heeded. Then there was started, somewhere or other, a rumor that the Messiah was coming—the Messiah whom immemorial tradition had declared would one day come, followed by all the great chiefs and warriors of the past, returned to life, to lead the Indians to victory over their white oppressors. This idea broke forth simultaneously in the minds of many tribes—of the Sioux in Dakota, of the Cherokees in Indian Territory, of the Apaches in Arizona. It spread like an epidemic. It was born of the wretchedness and need of the people, and it found believers everywhere. The Indians began holding religious gatherings, with wild ceremonies, commonly called 'ghost dances'."[39]

Dancing among the Sioux had started at Kicking Bear's camp, near Cheyenne. Kicking Bear, and Short Bull, with Porcupine, had made personal visits to the Messiah in Nevada, and had brought the doctrine and its secrets east with them. A few of Sitting Bull's men were in attendance at the Cheyenne dances and, on their return, they brought Kicking Bear back with them. Not only did Kicking Bear tell the glories of the new revelation to Sitting Bull, but deputized the Bull to conduct the dances in the area, and presented him with a decorated shirt which became the mantle of his apostleship. The Bull, a spiritual and meditative man to begin with, listened soberly to the new voice. In this doctrine, whose basic tenet was rebirth and return to glory of the American Indian, he recognized hope for his starving and beaten people, and in it he cannily sensed an opportunity to regain his old power and standing over them.

The Grand River camp soon became one of the most lively centers of the dance. With all the persuasion at their command, Kicking Bear and Sitting Bull set their task to spread the doctrine and the dance throughout the Sioux nation. Disciples were sent into the hills, to contact every clan. Not content with just local conversions, their agents visited the Shoshones, Blackfoot, Arapahoes, Gros Ventrias, the Oglalas, and every other tribe or clan of the Great Plains and Rocky Mountain area. A great opportunity to regain his once-powerful standing as a leader had come to the Bull, and he did all in his power to take advantage of it.

"Naturally superstitious, the Indians were ready for such an outpouring of their feelings in the form of a religious dance. Bull had always gained his greatest successes from his ability as a medicine man or diplomat, and he felt that the time for him to get his revenge on the other chiefs and on the Government had arrived. He at the start joined in with the ghost dancers, not shouting and dancing so much as inciting the others to the greatest activity in that line. When the Indians would go dancing around in a circle until they fell to the ground from giddiness and exhaustion, the wily old chief would take his place alongside of the fallen one, and, after a few words with him, would announce what visions of the Messiah and the coming again of the hunting grounds of the past had been witnessed, and the dance would be resumed with renewed vigor. Soon another would fall in a faint and the same programme would be gone through with."[40]

Out of it all, and just as he had hoped, Sitting Bull was emerging as high priest of the new religion that in a single year had swept America. In similar pattern to that experienced by every other great religion, corruptive influences had crept in in direct proportion to the distance its practitioners were removed from source of its truth and light. Wovoka's concepts of tolerance, meekness, and acceptance of the white man were rapidly giving way to intolerance, hatred and hoped-for retribution upon the enemy. The Messiah's fakery of inviolability in the face of gunfire became the basis for the "ghost shirts," made of buckskin or cotton and decorated with holy symbols, which the fanatical and hysterical Sioux under urging of such leaders as Short Bull, Kicking Bear, Big Foot and Sitting Bull, were now donning in countless numbers. Where Wovoka had specified that the sacred dance be continued only for five days or five nights at a period, the Bull's disciples continued on to the frenzy of madness and utter exhaustion. One thing was common to the whole movement, however, and that was the imminent dawn of the millennium, when the whites would fall from their thrones of power, and the Indian would emerge as the chosen ones. The Sioux, unlike Wovoka's Paiutes, began carrying their firearms into the dance, in the hope of a double blessing, and a surer means of bringing the prophecies to fruition.

The American government, especially the agency heads and the military, grew increasingly alarmed at the craze which had set tens of thousands of Indians to dancing throughout America. Since the Indians were stubbornly secretive about their new religion and, in the case of the Sioux, some of them were dusting off guns, little attempt was made to view the phenomena as strictly a religious revival spurred on by the defeat and misery of their charges. To white officials and panicky settlers, the ghost dance was a war dance. For the sake of peace and general order, it must immediately and ruthlessly be put down. In November 1890, the military were put in control over the Sioux.

Knowing that Sitting Bull was thoroughly mixed up in this latest Sioux "uprising," that General Nelson A. Miles, harried into action by a hysterical press, nervous agents, and frightened white settlers, would be forced to any measure to put quick stop to the craze, and that the wily old chief's life was actually in danger, a number of friendly emissaries visited him with the hope of turning him from this last great folly. Among these were a few well-meaning Christian missionaries, and Catherine Weldon, a wealthy Philadelphia widow and representative of the National Indian Defense Association, whose sympathy had already been so closely attuned to the Bull's welfare that she actually had spent weeks at the old chief's lodge. Gossipers and enemies had already labeled Catherine the Bull's "white squaw," but she continued fearlessly to defend him against his enemies, and at the same time to plead with him to renounce the ghost craze while there still was time. James McLaughlin, agent at Standing Rock, who hated Sitting Bull because of the subversive power he wielded, and because he stood as constant challenge to authority over the Sioux, at least went through the motions of attempting to dissuade him from his stubborn course. None had any degree of success in changing the Bull's conviction that the Messiah was coming to save the Indian, and that end of the world was imminent.

General Miles, not forgetting his first interview with Sitting Bull, in which the chief had defiantly declared, "God Almighty did not make me an agency Indian, and I'll fight and die fighting before any white man can make me an agency Indian," issued an immediate order for his arrest. Anticipating trouble, and with the hope of luring the Bull into custody by some ruse that would prevent him from again fleeing into the badlands with his recalcitrants, Colonel W. F. Cody, "Buffalo Bill," a friend of the Bull's from the time of his abortive exhibition tour, was asked by General Miles to execute the order. This order, which, if carried out, might have saved the life of the Sioux chief through a voluntary surrender to custody, was never carried into final execution. Sitting Bull would have gone any place Buffalo Bill might have suggested, unprotestingly and in the name of the friendship which existed between them. But Miles' order, for some inexplicable reason, was violently protested by Agent McLaughlin, who argued that the man whom Cody was to arrest by friendship, in reality was a crazed and armed fanatic.

Buffalo Bill, with a showman's flourish, and much publicity, arrived at the reservation, and made ready for his mission. Before it was effected, however, the decision was countermanded.[41] McLaughlin reported that the Bull was already preparing to move the seat of his operations into the badlands, where only a full-scaled army expedition could ever take him. No attempt was made to investigate the truth or falsity of this report, in the great haste now made to capture him. On Saturday, December 13, 1890, General Miles gave the order. Next morning, Sunday, from Fort Yates, Troops F and G, Eighth Cavalry, a company of infantry, and a detachment of twenty of McLaughlin's Indian police, resplendent in flashy blue uniforms and dazzling brass, started into the southwest to "get" Sitting Bull.

"A correspondent of *The Chicago Tribune* asserts that there was a quiet understanding between the officers of the Indian and military departments that it would be impossible to bring Sitting Bull to Standing Rock alive, and that if brought in nobody would know precisely what to do with him. Though under arrest he would be a source of great annoyance, and his followers would continue their dances and threats against the neighboring white settlers. There was, therefore, a complete understanding between the commanding officers and the Indian police that the slightest attempt to rescue the old medicine man should be a signal to send Sitting Bull to the happy hunting ground. That the Government authorities, civil as well as military, from President Harrison and General Miles down, preferred the death of the famous old savage to his capture whole-skinned, few persons in Dakota, Indian or white, had a doubt. It was felt that Sitting Bull's presence anywhere behind iron bars would be the cause of endless troubles, while should he fall a victim to the ready Winchester the thousands of Messiah-crazed ghost dancers would rudely realize that his medicine, which was to make them bullet-proof and yet could not save so great an oracle, must be worthless after all, and should be forsaken for the paths of peace."[42]

The Indian police, whom General Miles and the agencies had cannily drawn into military service by the hundreds, were anathema in the eyes of Sitting Bull and the older Sioux war chiefs who so valiantly had battled for the autonomy of the Sioux nation. For these young warriors to desert the great tradition in favor of the food and uniform of the enemy, was reprehensible in the extreme. The Bull hated the young, flashy, well-fed Indian police, or "Metal Breasts," as the lowest type of traitors to his people. And they, knowing his feelings, hated him.

These native soldiers formed the vanguard in the forty-mile march on the Bull's camp at Grand River, which they reached at Monday's dawn. Behind them came the cavalry command under Captain Fouchet, bringing with them the new and modern carriage-mounted machine-guns which the government was now providing border soldiers to cope with Indian "threats." Farther back, swinging along through the cold night, was the infantry, commanded by Colonel W. F. Drum. The well-fed, well-dressed military held pointed contrast to the ill-housed, starving Indian wretches they were moving upon, and who constituted such a threat to the peace and security of the nation.

In spite of the early hour, and the secrecy and speed of the expedition, the village had somehow been alerted. Lights were glowing in many of the cabins, and it was surmised that the Bull was planning an early exodus for himself and his people. Without hesitance the Metal Breasts, under command of Lieutenant Bullhead, rode directly to the chief's log cabin. Sitting Bull, at least, was asleep. The door was noisily hammered open with rifle butts, the dark room of the little house was quickly filled with men. The old chief was yanked naked from his bed, and commanded at rifle-point to dress.

At first the Bull willingly complied, and made every effort in the surging excitement and lamp-light to get into his clothes, and follow his captors. But the arrogance of the Metal Breasts quickly irked him. Instead of allowing him to dress in dignity, or his women to help him, they clung on to his half-clad body as though he were a coyote in a trap. The humiliation of it was finally too much to bear, and he firmed in anger. Eventually they shoved him, at gun-point, out into the yard, and someone went for his horse—the friendly old gray circus animal.

The camp, now aware that it was indeed a seizure of Sitting Bull by the Metal Breasts, poured armed warriors out of a dozen cabins and tipis. Soon the Indian police were facing an angry circle of Hunkpapa Sioux. Had Sitting Bull said the word, his people would have dispersed, and allowed Bullhead to peaceably accomplish the arrest. But the old chief, humiliated as never before in his life, was now past the point of cooperation. There were angry words, and protests from the Bull's sons and women. Suddenly the verbal uproar became a sputter of gunfire. Bullhead caught a bullet that sent him spinning to the ground. But in the instant that he went down, he fired the blast that killed Sitting Bull. Guns now flashed from every direction in the darkness. As dawn came, the ground was littered with the dead and dying. Sitting Bull, and his two sons, Blackbird and Crow Foot, were all dead. The latter was only twelve years of age. Mortally wounded was Bullhead, who had moved so brazenly against the chief. In the death struggle, the Bull's body had caught seven bullets from guns of the Metal Breasts. To save their scalps from the angered Hunkpapas, the police, with the exception of two who were riding hell-for-leather toward Fouchet's cavalry, had fled into Sitting Bull's cabin.

The white cavalry moved in, opened up with automatic guns and explosive shells upon the village. Too shocked and panic-stricken to resist, the Indians bolted for the river.

As a whole, the raid was a well-planned, dramatic, and effective move against the Messiah and his religion. Death of its most famous oracle was grim notice that the American people had at last come to bloody grips with those who had the temerity to practice it.

XIII

Bloody Pentecost

Now, there will be a tree sprout up, and there all the members of our religion and the tribe must gather. That will be the place where we see our dead relations.
                                                             —SHORT BULL.

THE SIOUX had a tradition of freedom too long for its people to give up a cause without a struggle. Death of Sitting Bull did not end the ghost dance, nor did it bring the "hostiles" into panicky surrender of their guns or their beliefs. Except for those Indians who camped close to Standing Rock or Pine Ridge for agency hand-outs, or joined the American military, starvation and want stalked the entire Sioux nation. The allotments, which Congress had stupidly cut, had not even yet arrived. Graft among the whites took a substantial portion of it, anyway. The buffalo and game were gone from the plains. Even the clothing, sent by missionary-minded people of America's great cities, were sold by agency men to white settlers, or those Indians rich enough to buy, with little of it ever distributed free to the Indians who so desperately needed it. The one great hope remained in the imminent millennium, which the Messiah had promised a broken and defeated people. Killing Sitting Bull had failed to extinguish it.

There was Big Foot's band of hostiles, who had gone into camp at Wounded Knee Creek. They openly and defiantly continued to dance the ghost dance, they refused to surrender themselves to the agency as other more peace-minded Sioux were doing, and they utterly refused to give up their arms or their horses, even when promised food to eat. After the tragic fate of Sitting Bull, this camp had come to the conclusion that they would all be put to death should they surrender their arms to the military. They preferred cold and starvation to submission. They danced with frenzied madness in the hope of hastening the heavenly manifestation which the Messiah had promised, and the earth's return to pristine glory before they all starved to death, or died like dogs at the hands of their enemies.

So the second decisive move was made by the military. Early on the morning of December 29, Big Foot's band of hostiles found themselves surrounded by an army of two battalions of 500 men each. Colonel George A. Forsyth, in command, fearing the Indians might offer resistance, or attempt to escape, mounted his Hotchkiss guns so they could rake the village if necessary. When all was in readiness, the command was given for the Indians to come out of their tipis. Frightened squaws and children moved to a spot behind the tipis, while the braves, under order, advanced reluctantly to the place designated by the command. There they were placed in half circle, the warriors squatting on the ground in front of the tipi of Big Foot. Their chief could not obey the summons. He lay in his bed, desperately ill with pneumonia.

The captives were ordered, by twenties, to go to their tents, get their guns, and surrender them. The first twenty returned with two rusty and useless guns. Infuriated, Major S. M. Whitside, ordered his dismounted cavalrymen to close in. Then a detachment of white soldiers went through the tents, coming back with forty rusty muzzle-loaders. The warriors, now convinced that they were to die, commenced in plaintive notes, their death chant. As the search continued, the song increased in tempo. Suddenly Yellow Bird, the medicine man, as signal that the new millennium at last was at hand, threw a handful of dust into the air— a symbol of the dust storm that was to bury all whites. One of the Sioux jerked a gun from beneath his blanket and fired. Instantly the other braves stood up, threw off their blankets and grabbed the weapons they had concealed beneath them. In the ghost shirts they wore, they had decided to sell their lives as dearly as possible. Rifles began to sputter. Those armed only with tomahawks or scalping knives, rushed the soldiers nearest them. But outnumbered four to one by the soldiery, it was hopeless from the start.

The fight lasted half an hour. The slaughter has few counterparts in history. With the Hotchkiss guns belching their explosive, flaming death upon the camp, the Indians died as bravely as any Sioux in history. Big Foot, raising himself from his bed amidst the carnage, crawled out of his tipi, and died with twenty bullets in his body. When most of the braves were finished, the battle-crazed soldiers turned their guns on the screaming, frightened women and children. While the wounded Indians, to their last breath, fought the soldiers who were pouring their deadly volleys in upon them, other soldiers chased down the fleeing squaws and children, killing anything that was Indian, with no thought as to whether it was man, child, woman, or whether it possessed any capabilities of resistance.

Not content with rifles and Hotchkiss guns and their lethal fire, the howitzers now opened point-blank upon the camp and its last fleeing Indians. Site of the camp was chewed into bloody mincemeat. When the massacre was finished, few Indians had escaped, and nearly three hundred lay dead—more than half of them women and children. But the braves, who died in their ghost shirts, had accounted for twenty-five soldiers, and had wounded that many more.

After the slaughter the army withdrew to Standing Rock, taking along its own dead and wounded. Not until three days later, New Year's Day, 1891, was a detachment of soldiers sent out to bury the Indian dead, and gather up the Indian wounded. During this time there had been a blizzard, and the bodies of the slaughtered men, women and children had been frozen to stiffness in their blood. All the warriors were grotesquely sprawled in death at the spot where they had made their stand, but the bodies of the women and children were found as far as two miles away, where the gun-happy soldiers had mowed them down. "A number of women and children were found still alive, but all badly wounded or frozen, or both, and most of them died after being brought in. Four babies were found alive under the snow, wrapped in shawls and lying beside their dead mothers, whose last thought had been of them. They were all badly frozen and only one lived . . . It is a commentary on our boasted Christian civilization that although there were two or three salaried missionaries at the agency not one went out to say a prayer over the poor mangled bodies of these victims of war."[43]

A long, deep trench was dug in the frozen earth. Into it was dumped the bodies of the Indians, as though they were cordwood or offal. Before being thrown into the pit, however, many of the warriors were stripped of their clothing and their ghost shirts, and in callous nakedness shoved into the burial trench without even the dignity of these vestments of the religion for which they had suffered martyrdom.

When it was all over the Sioux of Standing Rock agency marked the site of this unholy mass burial with a wire fence. Its posts, in memory of the cause for which they had died, and as last mark of defiance, was smeared with Wovoka's sacred red paint from far-away Nevada.

After the massacre of Wounded Knee there was some desultory "resistance" of the Sioux, but for the most part, cowed, whipped, and frightened at last, they surrendered at the agencies to accept whatever mercies and treatment their enemies might feel inclined to dole out to them.

The American military was right in its assumption that an object lesson as to the ineffectuality of the ghost shirt in turning away live bullets would have salutary effect on its wearers. Certainly it had not saved Sitting

Bull, his sons, or the hundreds who had laid down their lives at Wounded Knee. Many a Sioux lost heart in the religion, and at the same time, lost hope for the future of his people. But the dance continued, though, of necessity, in secret. The Sioux were still destitute and hungry. The Messiah had promised his millennium when the grass again grew green. The bravest among them could even yet hope.

From a military standpoint the massacre of Wounded Knee was a decisive victory. It stands as effectual end to the last Indian resistance in America. It taught, without equivocation to any disturbed Indian thinking, that might was right, and that submission was the only possible course to existence. The heart went out of the Indian world in those bloody closing hours of 1891. A hundred years of extermination and suppression of native beliefs by the Christian-minded Americans was crowned by the greatest and most dramatic purge of them all—Wounded Knee. To be acceptable, the Indian religion must first of all be of white origin. And by all means, even at the pain of death, its Messiah must be a white man. And because of the gallantry and dispatch by which this lesson was made known to the American Indian, eighteen soldiers received the Medal of Honor for their valor at the "battle" of Wounded Knee.[44]

XIV

MISUNDERSTOOD MESSIAH

He said that in the fall of the year the youth of all good people would be renewed, so that nobody would be more than forty years old, and that if they behaved themselves well after this the youth of everyone would be renewed in the spring. —PORCUPINE.

ONE OF the strangest features of the messianic craze which swept America during the 1890s was the fact that so little was known of the center core of the movement—the Messiah himself. The American military, and agents on scores of reservations, were taxed to hysteria in their attempts to obliterate the ghost dance, but all through the rage of public excitement Wovoka carried on unmolested in Nevada.

False Christs arose within the movement, hoping either to grasp a little of the notoriety to themselves, or to cash in on the credulity of both Indians and whites. At least one white man attempted entry into the religion as its celestial head, but apparently he bungled a bit in timing. The Sioux, hard-pressed from every side, were in a frenzy of indecision following the death of Sitting Bull. On December 22, 1890, General Miles' Indian police arrested, at Red Cloud's Camp near Pine Ridge, a man who claimed to be the Messiah. When they pulled his blanket off, however, he was discovered to be a white man. Interrogation revealed that, far from being Jesus, he was a vibrating Christian from Iowa by the name of Hopkins. With his disguise and his aura snatched away, he begged, in the interest of peace, to be allowed to go into the badlands to preach to the Sioux. Instead, the hard-pressed military escorted him off the reservation—but not before the disgusted Red Cloud had spat in his face, and had said: "You go home. You are no son of God."[45]

A more authentic Indian, but still an imposter, was Johnson Sides. Oddly, he was Paiute, but half-breed, and from the Walker Lake reservation in Nevada. Johnson, considerably younger than Wovoka, was educated, spoke perfect English, and apparently was shrewdly calculating. Where Wovoka stood in humbleness before his followers, there was nothing humble about Johnson. He stepped forward as claimant to the new revelation, gave interviews to the press, and in his own garb and trappings of the Messiah, even journeyed to Los Angeles and other cities. More than one writer was taken in by the effrontery of Johnson Sides. At the height of the Sioux troubles General Miles received a letter from an army officer in Los Angeles concerning an interview with this self-styled Messiah. "Last spring an Indian called and said he would like to speak to the commander," the letter stated. "I took him into the room, and he gave me a history of himself. He said his name was Johnson Sides; that he was known as the Peacemaker among all Indians and whites of Nevada, where he lived.

"To substantiate his statement he showed me a medal which he carried strung around his neck, on which was a legend to the effect that he was presented with the medal by some Christian society for his efforts toward doing good to his fellowmen, whether red or white.

"He could talk very good English, was dressed like an ordinary laborer, but had the Indian's way of wearing his hair. He told me he knew the Bible; that he was desirous of making peace with everyone, and that is why he was named Peacemaker. He said that Indians had come from far and near to see him, and he pulled out a pipe, such as are made by Northern Indians, which pipe was recognized as having come from either Montana or Dakota. Johnson Sides said it came from Dakota, and the kind of clay of which it was made could not be found in Nevada . . . He mentioned the names of the Indians who had visited him, and the tribes to which they belonged; also gave the time they had called."[46]

But with the death of Sitting Bull and the Sioux blood-letting at Wounded Knee, the Messiahs, pretenders and real, now either sought complete anonymity or went underground. Not even a divine personage would want to head up a religious movement that had brought so insufferable and far-reaching a tragedy upon its peoples.

When the news of this bloody December reached Wovoka, he refused to believe it. The doctrine he had taught his people, and the revelation he had imparted to his visitors from afar, had nothing whatever to do with bloodshed. "You must not fight," he had admonished. "Do no harm to anyone. Do right always." Repeatedly he had told them not to bait the white man to anger; to accept with meekness and humility the white man's yoke—up until the coming hour when the Great God would right the injustices, heal the wounds, and return a resurrected world to the Indian. "Do not refuse to work for the whites, and do not make any trouble with them," he had cautioned. But trouble had come; and, being so far outside the realm of probable reaction to the doctrine, he refused to believe it had any connection whatever with the new religion.

But news continued to confirm the fact that his ghost dance had been the very core of the Sioux troubles, and that a concerted effort by the United States Government was everywhere being made to suppress it. When finally he came to realize the enormity of the tragedy that had come out of the once simple religion he had preached, and the fact that he faced the possibility of having to answer for it all, he was shaken to the marrow. At every opportunity he explained that the eastern tribes had perverted the meaning of the doctrine, had made a thing out of it that he had not taught, and that the ghost shirts and their war implications were things concocted by them and added to the ritual without his consent.

Sorrowed, and oppressed with guilt, he left family and friends, and went to the holy mountain to meditate and pray. When he returned to Mason Valley, it was to find not only pathetic letters from the tribal leaders in the east, confirming the massacre in all its bloody details, and either censuring him for having brought it on, or begging him to put speedy end to the world as it was, to invoke the prophecy, and bring down heaven's promised judgment on the white man and his murderous works. Present, too, was a white man from Washington to see him—a great American scout by the name of Arthur Chapman, who, under instructions from the War Department, had been sent to interview the Messiah, and to forward the information he obtained to the east.[47]

Assured that Chapman had no intention of arresting him or hauling him to a white man's prison, Wovoka carried on a cautious interview with his visitor. As always, even though he had fluent command of the English language, Wovoka insisted their conversations be in Paiute. This put a definite handicap on Chapman, but with the aid of a neighboring rancher who spoke both languages, enough information was wrung out of the canny and cautious Messiah that Chapman could forward on to Washington the first understandable and authentic report on the strange religion that had inflamed a continent. It took four days to conclude the talks, throughout which Wovoka insisted on making plain the fact that the thing he preached had peace and brotherly love as its basis, that it shunned the very thought of bloodshed and rebellion, and that the orgiastic trances and ghost shirts, so markedly a part of the eastern picture, had never been known to the dance as introduced and conducted in Mason Valley. He insisted on the authenticity of his own vision, the profound conviction that he was the Chosen One, and admitted that he was subject to trances and spiritual seizures, but he repudiated any hint of responsibility for those cor-

THE FROZEN BODY OF CHIEF BIG FOOT

Photograph taken at Wounded Knee, several days after the massacre.

—*From the Reynolds collection;*
courtesy of J. E. Reynolds.

MASS BURIAL OF BIG FOOT'S BAND

After the massacre by American troops of the Sioux Ghost Dancers at Wounded Knee—one of the most brutal exterminations in Indian history. Drawing by Josepha Newcomb, after a photograph.

—*Courtesy Bureau of American Ethnology.*

ruptive additions that were leading so many of his disciples astray.

Chapman took his departure, but left behind him a worried Messiah. Winter's grip was upon the Nevada's mesas, snow was upon the sage, and the river was iced. With the chill winds howling down from the mountains, there was little opportunity or inclination for dancing groups to assemble. And it was well, for Wovoka needed a time to ponder the complexity of problems now facing him. He was convinced that the government had at last put its finger on him as leader of the movement, and that in spite of explanations and denials, they would eventually hold him responsible for the Sioux rebellion, the bloodshed, and the pugnacity and ferment now boiling within the various tribes.

Too, the coming of the new grass was the time he had personally set for the breakup of the world. The passing of the winter would set upon him the necessity of either bringing the great miracle to pass, acceptably postponing it, or standing discredited as a prophet before his people. These problems were worrisome enough, without having to face jail or death for the bloody happenings in Dakota. He had tried to explain the doctrine as he had taught it, against the perversions and excesses that had brought about the eastern tragedies. But he had little faith that Chapman or any other government man would stand in his defense at Washington.

As winter receded, and "God's year" of 1891 crept into the green of spring, visitors from eastern and local tribes again made their way into Mason Valley, but in diminished numbers as compared with the year previous. As a part of caution, the worried Messiah changed his dancing and preaching locale closer to the lake and farther away from the white settlement which had grown up in the valley. White men no longer were a welcome part of the ritual, either as spectators or participants, and a number of the dances were arbitrarily broken up by Our Father when white men, impelled by curiosity, dropped in to view the spectacle.

In his visitors from other tribes Wovoka sensed a new fear and anxiety. Passes away from tribal areas were no longer casually granted by the agents to traveling Indians. Most of those who now sought Wovoka were virtual fugitives from their reservations, absent without permission, subject to arrest by any agent who found them outside the limits of their respective tribal lands. Since the Sioux troubles, and impelled by an official determination to break up the ghost craze at all costs, the Indians of America had become virtual prisoners within their tribal confines. It now was a dangerous thing to make the holy pilgrimage to Nevada.

Indian jails on more than one reservation were well stuffed with those who had tried and failed.

In his visitors Wovoka sensed new fright and new anxiety—in addition to the natural fear of being caught and imprisoned for being so far from home without agency credentials. "How long, Our Father," they implored him, "before the world breaks up, and our people who are dead, come back to us?" And the only answer Wovoka could give to their anxious hearts was the charge that all things depended upon the purification, and the dance, and that only the proper and continued practice of the ritual could force the hand of God to bring about these promised wonders. "But white soldiers have come," came the new and perplexing revealment. "They will shoot us if we dance." To this there was no proper answer, other than the promise that if Indians behaved themselves, the soldiers might soon leave. And to Wovoka there was a slight satisfaction that if the great wonders did not come to pass in this, the millennial year, white soldiers could properly be held to blame for interfering with that thing which alone could bring about the colossal heavenly upheaval.

In more than one of his visitors Our Father began to sense a note of skepticism, almost wholly absent in the long lines of visitors who had come to him the year previous. Some of them were argumentative, querulous, and even openly questioned his powers and his claims. No longer was blind acceptance the rule. It was taking diplomacy, tact, and a smattering of theatrics to maintain that once firm hold on his followers.

After the dances and the councils Wovoka would disappear. No longer was he available to visitors in the wikiup of his family. Throughout the year he shunned white men and white settlements. There was constant worry in his heart that white soldiers or agents might come to arrest him as nominal head of the movement which had come to such grief. One thing, however, he could not dodge, and that was the United States mail. Indians from the east, through their Carlisle-trained scribes, sent money and letters to Mason Valley postoffice, still begging him for holy red paint, magpie feathers, and any part of the apparel which had touched the body of Our Father. On hats and shirts alone he did a lucrative business. He had been in the habit of buying shirts and Stetsons from Dyer's Store, wearing them long enough for the spiritual contact to permeate them, and then mailing them east to the tribal leaders. Established price for hats was twenty dollars. In these transactions, young Ed Dyer, the energetic proprietor who spoke fluent and understandable Paiute acted as willing amanuensis and translator.[48] Patiently he answered the Messiah's dictated correspondence, and handled the bothersome traffic in holy paint and feathers, including even the more bulky problems of hats.

Through the years Wovoka had continued to keep a close and running friendship with the Wilsons, but after his meteoric rise in the religious world, and with it the absolute necessity of someone to write letters for him, and to read his sizable incoming mail out of the white man's language in which they were written, he had come to a deep dependence on Ed Dyer for this all-important chore. A warm friendship had developed with Dyer, who accepted him without question, criticism or ridicule. Now, irrespective of the fact that he had exiled himself from white men, and had made himself all but inaccessible to his own people, the mail continued to arrive at Mason Valley postoffice. This created the necessity of an occasional visit to the white man's world, and one which he could not possibly avoid. But Dyer was friendly and discreet. Under cover of darkness the ubiquitous Messiah would go to Dyer's home, and uncomplainingly Dyer would open the store, read the mail to Wovoka, write down whatever the Messiah dictated in answer, and take care of the shipments of holy objects from Our Father's wagon or saddle-bags. To keep ahead of schedule it was necessary to purchase hats and shirts in advance—which

Dyer kept in proper stock and proper size—so that Our Father could lend to them the proper and necessary touch of his body through at least nominal wearing. Wovoka appreciated Dyer's friendship and help through this trying and worrisome period. Businesswise, Dyer in turn appreciated these visits from Wovoka. And, sensing the problems of his Indian friend, kept the matter discreetly to himself.

In this fashion the year 1891 wore on through its summer and into another winter. Then, quite without warning, the Messiah had another visitor from Washington.

James Mooney, of the United States Bureau of Ethnology, had taken a deep interest in the ghost dance religion almost from its inception. Unlike the American military, and the almost criminally blind and stupid politicians who administered Indian affairs, Mooney recognized this new spiritual craze as one of the great religious movements of history—a movement which in eighteen months had influenced the lives and thinking of tens of thousands of the world's population. Realizing the necessity of studying this phenomenon at closest possible hand, without reliance on distorted and biased military and agency reports, Mooney set off on a journey which took him into twenty tribes, consumed nearly 32,000 miles of travel and almost two years of time. Without the masterful studies of this devoted man, and the reports which he later published, little actual data could ever have been gathered on Wovoka and his religion.[49]

XV

THE GREAT WHITE FATHER SEEKS THE MESSIAH

I have told you that this would come to pass in two seasons, but since the whites are interfering so much, I will advance the time from what my father above told me to do, so the time will be shorter. Therefore you must not be afraid of anything. Some of my relations have no ears, so I will have them blown away. —SHORT BULL.

MOONEY'S personal journey in search of the Messiah, following his prolonged study of the ghost dance phenomena in the various prairie tribes, began from Washington in November 1891. "After a few days with the Omaha and Winnebago in Nebraska, and a longer stay with the Sioux at Pine Ridge, where traces of the recent conflict were still fresh on every hand, I crossed over the mountains and finally arrived at Walker Lake reservation in Nevada,"[50] Mooney explains.

At the reservation agency was confirmed a fact, previously noted by letter, that little was known about Wovoka *alias* Jack Wilson, his messianic office, or the ghost dance proper. Agent C. C. Warner seemed either ignorant or not interested in the fact that the great dances, participated in by delegates from numerous American tribes, had been going on and were still going on in Mason Valley, only forty miles northwest of his office.[51] And while this agent slept out his tenure in Nevada, with the Messiah and fountainhead of the greatest religious ferment in Indian history virtually under his thumb, the newspapers and magazines of America were afire with stories of the "great uprising" about which no authentic data was to be had, and which had already brought two bloody massacres to its participants. The only thing clearly known at the agency was that Jack Wilson appeared to be a harmless dreamer, known to associate with the whites, and the nominal leader of Mason Valley's faction of Paiutes and their dances. It was known also that in the last year he had studiously avoided any visits to the agency, or any contacts whatever with governmental officialdom.

Inquiry disclosed the fact that Wovoka's uncle, Charley Sheep, lived near the agency, "so I sought him out and made his acquaintance," says Mooney. "He spoke tolerable—or rather intolerable—English, so that we were able to get along together without an interpreter, a fact which brought us into closer sympathy, as an interpreter is generally at best only a necessary evil. As usual, he was very suspicious at first, and inquired minutely as to my purpose. I explained to him that I was sent by the government to the various tribes to study their customs and learn their dances and songs; that I had obtained a good deal from other tribes and now wanted to learn some songs and stories of the Paiute, in order to write them down so that the white people could read them. In a casual way I then offered to show him the pictures of some of my Indian friends across the mountains, and brought out the photos of several Arapaho and Cheyenne who I knew had recently come as delegates to the Messiah. This convinced him that I was all right, and he became communicative. The result was that we spent about a week together in the wikiups, surrounded always by a crowd of interested Paiutes, discussing the old stories and games, singing Paiute songs, and sampling the seed mush and roasted piñon nuts. On one of these occasions, at night, a medicine-man was performing his incantations over a sick child on one side of the fire while we were talking on the other. When the ice was well thawed, I cautiously approached the subject of the ghost songs and dance, and, as confidence was now established, I found no difficulty in obtaining a number of the songs, with a description of the ceremonial. I then told Charley that, as I had taken part in the dance, I was anxious to see the Messiah and get from him some medicine-paint to bring back to his friends among the eastern tribes. He readily agreed to go with me and use his efforts with his nephew to obtain what was wanted."[52]

The two men, James Mooney and Charley Sheep, now warm friends, took the train to Wabuska, rented horses, and rode from there the twelve miles south-westerly to the Mason Valley settlement—the settlement which was destined soon to become the modern town of Yerington. There Charley Sheep took Mooney immediately to Edward Dyer, the closest white friend and confidant Wovoka had in the village. Dyer readily disclosed the fact that the Messiah had secluded himself at Pine Grove, and was extremely cagy about visitors—especially government men.

By now Mooney had learned a number of interesting things about Wovoka, among which was the fact that, should he be fortunate enough to win an audience with Our Father, that any utterances pertaining to the strange religion would be in Paiute—a condition Wovoka had maintained from the first. Dyer spoke fluent Paiute, and Mooney had need of him as interpreter. When Dyer, in turn, was convinced that Mooney contemplated no arrest or harm to his friend, he agreed to accompany the party in search of him—which, with the addition of a driver for a rented team and wagon, now numbered four men.

The Great White Father Seeks The Messiah

On New Year's Day of 1892 they set out on the twelve mile journey to Pine Grove. It was complicated and impeded by a heavy and unusual winter storm, which had piled its snow into bothersome drifts that taxed the strength of the horses and hindered their progress up the wintry mountain slopes where the Messiah had chosen to do his hiding.

"Soon after leaving the settlement," Mooney tells of the journey, "we passed the dance ground with the brush shelters still standing. We met but few Indians on the way. After several miles we noticed a man at some distance from the road with a gun across his shoulder. Dyer looked a moment and then exclaimed, 'I believe that's Jack now!' The Indian Charley Sheep thought so, too, and pulling up our horses he shouted some words in the Paiute language. The man replied. and sure enough it was the Messiah, hunting jack rabbits. At his uncle's call he soon came over.

"As he approached I saw that he was a young man, a dark full-blood, compactly built, and taller than the Paiute generally, being nearly 6 feet in height. He was well dressed in white man's clothes, with the broad-brimmed white felt hat common in the west, secured on his head by means of a beaded ribbon under the chin . . . He wore a good pair of boots. His hair was cut off square on a line below the base of the ears, after the manner of his tribe. His countenance was open and expressive of firmness and decision, but with no marked intellectuality. The features were broad and heavy, very different from the thin, clear-cut features of the prairie tribes.

"As he came up he took my hand with a strong, hearty grasp, and inquired what was wanted. His uncle explained matters, adding that I was well acquainted with some of his Indian friends who had visited him a short time before, and was going back to the same people. After some deliberation he said that the whites had lied about him and he did not like to talk to them; some of the Indians had disobeyed his instructions and trouble had come of it, but as I was sent by Washington and was a friend of his friends, he would talk with me. He was hunting now, but if we would come to his camp that night he would tell us about his mission."[53]

The four wayfarers, elated by the good fortune that had come to them, put in at the nearest farm house. By night time it was freezing, and they started out through the darkness toward the mountain camp of Wovoka. They suffered a hectic experience reaching there, being lost for several hours in the snowy sagebrush before finally arriving at the three or four little wikiups, within one of which the Messiah waited.

"On entering through the doorway," Mooney explains, "we found ourselves in a circular lodge made of bundles of tulé rushes laid over a framework of poles, after the fashion of the thatched roofs of Europe, and very similar to the grass lodges of the Wichita. The lodge was only about 10 feet in diameter and about 8 feet in height, with sloping sides, and was almost entirely open above, like a cone with the top cut off . . . In the center, built directly on the ground, was a blazing fire of sagebrush, upon which fresh stalks were thrown from time to time, sending up a shower of sparks into the open air . . . Sitting or lying around the fire were half a dozen Paiute, including the Messiah and his family, consisting of his young wife, a boy about 4 years of age, of whom he seemed very fond, and an infant. It was plain that he was a kind husband and father, which was in keeping with his reputation among the whites for industry and reliability. . .

"Wovoka received us cordially and then inquired more particularly as to my purpose in seeking an interview. His uncle entered into a detailed explanation, which stretched out to a preposterous length, owing to a peculiar conversational method of the Paiute. Each statement by the older man was repeated at its close, word for word and sentence by sentence, by the other, with the same monotonous inflection. This done, the first speaker signified by a grunt of approval that it had been correctly repeated, and then proceeded with the next statement, which was duly repeated in like manner.

"At last he signified that he understood and was satisfied, and then in answer to my questions gave an account of himself and his doctrine, a great part of the interpretation being by Dyer, with whom he seemed to be on intimate terms."[54]

The lengthy and prolonged interview which followed was one of candor and honesty. James Mooney, through skillful and sympathetic use of the tools of mutual acquaintance, mutual understanding, and above all, tact, was able to draw from Our Father a true and understandable account of what Wovoka actually taught, and how the ghost dance religion came to be. Without the dedicated effort of this man, in his determined resolve to winnow out the facts from an immense cordage of hate and misunderstanding, little of truth would ever have been known of the greatest Indian religious upheaval in history. Had the Indian office and the United States Army traveled the same course through its hysteria, into a basic understanding of the great force which so mysteriously had moved across the face of the land, there would have been no deadly reprisals to add mockery to an already long and unenviable record of broken faith.

GRAVE OF THE MESSIAH
The wooden slab which marks the grave of Wovoka (Jack Wilson), in the Indian burial ground at Schurz, Nevada.

—*Paul Bailey photo.*

LAST RESTING PLACE OF WOVOKA (JACK WILSON) AND HIS WIFE MARY

Indian burial ground, Schurz, Nevada, approximately twenty-five miles from the scene of Wovoka's religious activities.

—*Paul Bailey photo.*

In the Mooney talks the Messiah revealed his age, at the time, as about thirty-five years, the date being fixed from the great battle of 1860, which occurred between the Paiutes and the whites, at Pyramid Lake.[55] He claimed to be about four years old at the time. He told of his father, Tävibo, a petty chief, a dreamer, and a man, like himself, invulnerable. His own proper name, he explained, was Wovoka, or Wüvoka, "The Cutter," but that since his rise to prominence, he was now assuming the name of his paternal grandfather, Kwohitsauq, or "Big Rumbling Belly." To add further confusion to nomenclature, he revealed the fact that he had been taken into the family of David Wilson, who in turn had given him the anglicized name of Jack Wilson—the name the whites invariably had preferred calling him.

He explained that he was married at about twenty years of age, and for a time after that had continued to work for Wilson. "He had given the dance to his people about four years before," Mooney wrote, "but had received his great revelation about two years previously. On this occasion 'the sun died' [was eclipsed] and he fell asleep in the daytime and was taken up to the other world. Here he saw God, with all the people who had died long ago engaged in their oldtime sports and occupations, all happy and forever young. It was a pleasant land and full of game. After showing him all, God told him he must go back and tell his people they must be good and love one another, have no quarreling, and live in peace with the whites; that they must work, and not lie or steal; that they must put away all the old practices that savored of war; that if they faithfully obeyed his instructions they would at last be reunited with their friends in this other world, where there could be no more death or sickness or old age. He was then given the dance which he was commanded to bring to his people. By performing this dance at intervals, for five consecutive days each time, they would secure this happiness to themselves and hasten the event. Finally God gave him control over the elements so that he could make it rain or snow or be dry at will, and appointed him his deputy to take charge of affairs in the west, while 'Governor Harrison' would attend to matters in the east, and he, God, would look after the world above. He [Wovoka] then returned to earth and began to preach as he was directed, convincing the people by exercising the wonderful powers that had been given him."[56]

In his interview with Mooney, as in his previous one with Chapman, Wovoka refused to assume any responsibility for the ghost shirt which had become so prevalent among the Sioux, and so much a part of their dance ritual.[57] The trances and spiritual orgies which had infected the dance among the eastern tribes were not a part of the ritual as he had taught it in Nevada, he explained. And, hostility to the whites was no part of his doctrine, which was one of universal peace.

Mooney continued to press for a revealment of Wovoka's actual underlying feelings regarding the thing he had let loose in the world. "While he repudiated almost everything for which he had been held responsible in the east, he asserted positively that he had been to the spirit world and had been given a revelation and message from God himself, with full control over the elements."

"I accepted his statements with several grains of salt," Mooney states, "but on the whole he seemed to be honest in his belief and his supernatural claims, although, like others of the priestly functions, he occasionally resorts to cheap trickery to keep up the impression as to his miraculous powers. From some of the reports he is evidently an expert sleight-of-hand performer. He makes no claim to be Christ, the Son of God, as has been so often asserted in print. He does claim to be a prophet who has received a divine revelation. I could not help feeling that he was sincere in his repudiation of a number of the wonderful things attributed to him, for the reason that he insisted so strongly on other things fully as trying to the faith of a white man. He made no arguments and advanced no proofs, but said simply that he had been with God, as though the statement no more admitted of controversy than the proposition that 2 and 2 are 4."[58]

"In subsequent conversations," says Mooney, "he added a few minor details in regard to his vision and his doctrine. He asked many questions in regard to the eastern tribes whose delegates had visited him, and was pleased to learn that the delegates from several of these tribes were my friends. He spoke particularly of the large delegation—about twelve in number—from the Cheyenne and Arapaho, who had visited him the preceding summer and taken part in the dance with his people. Nearly all the members of this party were personally known to me, and the leader, Black Coyote, whose picture I had with me and showed to him, had been my principal instructor in the Ghost Dance among the Arapaho. While this fact put me on a more confidential footing with Wovoka, it also proved of great assistance in my further investigation on my return to the prairie tribes, as, when they were satisfied from my statements and the specimens which I had brought back that I had indeed seen and talked with the Messiah, they were convinced that I was earnestly desirous of understanding their religion aright, and from that time spoke freely and without reserve."[59]

After a little persuasion Mooney succeeded in getting consent for a photograph—the first one ever taken of the Messiah. In preparation Wovoka knotted a handkerchief about his neck, fastened an eagle feather at his right elbow, and carefully laid his wide-brimmed Stetson across his knee. All these items had spiritual significance, and Wovoka cannily insisted they be a part of the picture. As souvenirs to take back on his return to the plains Indians, Mooney obtained from Wovoka a rabbit-skin blanket, some piñon nuts, some magpie tail-feathers, and a quantity of the sacred and miraculous red paint so essential to the ghost dance religion. On the friendliest of terms, James Mooney took his departure from the Messiah, to return once more to the Indian Territory in further study of the strange religion. And, most important of all, he took away from Nevada the clearest knowledge any white man possessed of the character, personality, and doctrine of Wovoka, the son of Tävibo.

XVI

Last Days

He told us not to quarrel or fight or strike each other, or shoot one another; that the whites and Indians were to be all one people. —PORCUPINE.

THE MESSIANIC doctrine of Wovoka remained a persistent thing among the Indians of America for a decade after Wounded Knee, but time, and the uncertain nature of prophecy, brought final neglect, loss of interest, and vanishment of hope to its converts. The corruptive additives of the plains Indians likewise contributed to its disrepute among the more sober-thinking tribesmen, and when the great millennium failed to appear, in spite of persistency and frenzy of the dance, Wovoka's religion followed the same pattern into eclipse suffered by those other "end-of-the-world" cults which flowered and died among the white men.

It is doubtful that the heavy pressure brought to bear against it by the Indian Office and military had anything to do with its gradual abandonment by the tens of thousands who were its converts. History has never failed to show that to persecute a religion is to make it strong. The craze was at its very height when danger was the greatest and, had its converts remained fired with its zeal, it would have taken the bloody extermination of a race to have obliterated it. Humans, red or white, just do not alter thinking at the point of a gun. And the strength of any religion is nurtured by the blood of its martyrs.

Had Wovoka's religion a timelessness and a staying quality, Sitting Bull and the dead of Wounded Knee Massacre would have risen as its saints. But the Messiah himself, in setting positive dates for the great millennium, had signed a death warrant for the faith. No Indians ever danced with greater zeal than did the Sioux, but the barren earth remained the same, the buffalo did not return, and the white man continued to be just as hard, avaricious and cruel as ever. Unlike the white man's prophets, who left such things to dreamy conjecture, Wovoka had date-stamped the Great Event. Time, and time alone, was his undoing.

Visitors continued to come to Wovoka's Nevada Galilee, but in sharply decreasing numbers as the years rolled along, and he was forced to alter his prophecies to fit the shape of events. When it became apparent that the government itself was losing interest, that there seemed no further inclination on officialdom's part to jail him as a trouble-maker, the Messiah came out of hiding, and once more was seen in the vicinity of white men. The settlers of Mason Valley, their generation of children, and the newer townsmen, cared less and less about the strange Indian in their area who had visitors, and was connected in some vague way with the recent excitement of the ghost dance. In the new town of Yerington, which grew up around Mason Valley post office, he was never called by his Indian name of Wovoka, but was throughout his life known simply as Jack Wilson, some sort of head man to the Walker River Paiutes.

As long as Edward Dyer kept store in Yerington, Wovoka continued his useful friendship with this kindly white man who spoke Paiute, wrote letters for him, and did not scoff at a prophet whose star was waning. Although the eastern tribes were losing all hope of a millennium, and the Messiah stood discredited in their eyes because he had failed to set their sad world in order, Wovoka never ceased to do a lively business in magpie feathers and the sacred red ochre from the vicinity of the holy mountain, which their medicine men and chiefs now considered as almost standard equipment to their calling. He even shipped an occasional hat to those who persisted in believing on its

efficacy and charm to the wearer, though these transactions grew fewer with the years.

By the turn of the century the sphere of his influence
had once more receded to the Nevada area where he
was immediately known and respected. It became increasingly difficult for him to gather together, even
among his own people, enough interested ones to form
a circle for the stately ghost dance. Though he passion-
ately argued for its necessity, that God Himself had
willed it, there were those now who smiled indulgently
upon Our Father, and seemed unmoved by his elo-
quence. And mere casual acceptance was the last thing
Wovoka desired.

In its newness the 20th Century brought with it a
white man's world—bristling and alive with growth
and promise, completely and totally uninterested in
the Indian and his problem. Tribes, ruthlessly com-
pressed into geographical fractions of their once great
domains, or moved out to sterile areas where even a
horned toad would find it difficult to survive, were,
now that they were subjugated and silenced, dismissed
from thought, and left entirely to the good or bad
management of the Indian Office. Indicative of the
great oblivion is the fact that not a single Indian personality emerged as newsworthy enough to command

even a passing interest in the white man's great machine age.

Wovoka, son of Tävibo, dropped from even the
memories of those who had dealt with him. The once
millennial-minded Mormons lost interest in him along
with their discovery that the earth was a pretty solid
place after all, that there was money to be made, that
their own looked for Messiah's second coming was conveniently delayed while they prospered, and the
Book of Mormon promises to the Indians was neither
an easy thing to put over, nor an advent likely to be
accomplished in the 20th Century's machine age. Wovoka, so far as the world at large was concerned, was
as dead as Sitting Bull.

But in his little Nevada Galilee, where he finished
out his life in comparative obscurity, he was not entirely a prophet without honor. In the dwindling band
of Paiutes at Walker River, there still lived those
who called him "Our Father." Even though they were
too busy working white men's farms and industries
to be much interested in the circles of his dance, his
trances, or the thunderous prophecies he occasionally
gave forth, they still rendered him the respect of his
calling. In rabbit hunts, he still rode in dignity in a
wagon pulled by good horses. And, among the more
faithful ones, a tithe of their fish, game and earnings

was rendered him—sufficient to take care of his mundane needs. But Wovoka moved through it all in sorrow.

As civilization began to take the hazards out of the calling of tribal medicine man, and there was little danger now that one would be put to death for his failures in healing, he began more than ever to essay that role. In addition to the chants and hand- and breath-manipulations which were standard equipment among Paiute healers, he began gathering herbs and roots. These, with his feathers and red paint, he continued to sell throughout his lifetime—an insistent advocate of their effectiveness in warding off disease and the evil spirits that plagued mankind.

But the sorrow of his rejection as a prophet, the humiliation of having been cast aside and forgotten, ate deep into the heart of the Messiah. Externally, at least, he showed no bitterness. He did not turn to drink, with which so many of his tribesmen drowned their senses of defeat, inadequacy and despair. Instead, in the gentleness and patience of the real Jesus, he strove to teach and counsel his little band of Mason Valley Paiutes into decent and productive lives.

He never ceased to preach the necessity of Indian acceptance of the white man, and cooperation with him—until that day when wrongs would be righted, and the Indian once more would rise out of degradation. Jack Wilson became the source through which Mason Valley ranches and Yerington tradesmen sought their Indian labor. During harvest season the Messiah himself would lend a hand to the Wilsons or other ranchers he especially favored. Even today in that area he is better remembered as plain Jack Wilson, friendly Paiute head man, than a messianic phenomenon who had churned the Indian world into a frenzy.

But the sorrow of his defeat settled in lines of hurt about his gentle eyes. Age unmistakably brought the marks of inner suffering to a face already gentled by time. Those who knew him testify that he never ceased to grieve for those who had died in the name of the religion he had introduced—misguided martyrs though he knew them to be. The unending ache in his soul grew out of the great riddle—why should a religion which taught only hope, peace and love, have brought the last great carnage of bloodshed and death to the very Indians he was striving to help? And why, now, was this religion all but forgotten? The United States Government was no longer under moral necessity to chase down the instigator of the ghost dance revolt. By his plain and simple predictions, the father of it all had rendered his own judgment. And throughout his lifetime the riddle of it wracked Wovoka's soul.

With the full settling up of Mason Valley, the aging Messiah moved his wife and family into the ramshackle Indian community an indifferent government had set up south and west of Yerington. Of his numerous progeny, few had lived. And, as customary with Paiutes, with their death, especially as infants or children, they were spoken of no more. The son, which Mooney had taken such special notice of, died early in childhood. For a time it appeared that Wovoka, and his loyal and devoted wife Mary, might rear the final three daughters—Daisy, Ida and Alice—to maturity. But in the end, only Alice lived into full adulthood. Through all the vicissitudes of his strange lifetime, Mary was companion to his success and his sorrow, and, insofar as any Indian wife can be, comforter and confidant.

Oddly, too, through the waning years of his life, there was never a complete cessation of belief, in the Indian community, at least, that Wovoka was invulnerable, would live on indefinitely, and would never taste death. In Mason Valley, as a man among the Paiutes, he was still something mysterious and special.

In 1926 Colonel Tim McCoy, lifelong student and friend of the American Indian, star of motion pictures and wild west shows, deliberately sought out the aged and rejected Messiah. He found him in his little hut in the Paiute village, both friendly and willing to talk. "I found a man unusually vigorous for nearly seventy years of age," McCoy states. "He seemed robust, and at least twenty years younger. He talked readily of the ghost dance religion, and of the great visits he once had with the tribal leaders from the east. He still talked of the coming millennium, in which the Indian would be given a new earth to dwell upon. He still emphatically declared that he had visited God, and had talked to Him. And he appeared to have the impression that he would never die."[60]

McCoy not only obtained one of the rare photographs of Wovoka, but attended with him a Paiute dance at the Pyramid Lake reservation. Here the Messiah was called upon to attempt the healing of a tribesman dying of tuberculosis. In the ancient Paiute manner, the Messiah put his lips to the bony chest of the sick man, and drew out the evil that was distressing him. Two nights later the sick man was dancing with his people.

But six years later, irrespective of belief or declaration of invulnerability, the Messiah came to a quiet and peaceful end. Mary had died a month previous, and the loss of her had all but crushed him. And now, in his own death, instead of ten thousand Indians chanting his song of passing, there was present in the little house Wovoka's daughter Ida, and a grandson,

Dennis Bender. The *Mason Valley News,* which for over a quarter of a century had chronicled all the happenings and trivia of the white residents of the valley, had not a line in mention of the passing of what was probably the valley's most noted citizen. As for the Mason Valley Paiutes, they were shocked and confused. They had come to accept Jack Wilson as invulnerable— the one man among them who would never know death.

In the weedy, rocky cemetery of the little Indian town of Schurz, not far from Yerington, the Messiah, with scarcely a mourner, was lowered to the grave he once claimed he would never see. A wooden slab, painted with the simple words, "JACK WILSON, DIED SEPT. 20, 1932, AGE 74," was set up as marker, and the man and his grave turned over to the Nevada desert and promptly forgotten.

But never will be forgotten the amazing thing he deliberately or accidentally brought forth. Whether divinely inspired prophet, or opportunist and faker, there can be no denial of his accomplishments. In point of time, and numerical count of its converts, the thing he preached must be rated as one of the world's great religious movements. When Christian evangelists of the white race had spent a century attempting to convert the American Indian, without having made a dent in their "pagan" beliefs, an obscure native prophet, in an obscure valley of Nevada, preaches a doctrine which, in letters of fire, sweeps a continent. White men, because they had little hand in its conception, and because its ritual sprung out of a mixture of stark paganism and biblical promise, will doubtless feel it necessary to look down their collective noses at Wovoka and the things he preached. But no man in honesty can claim its tenets any more a strain upon credulity than the hundreds of Christian sects, battling for supremacy among themselves, and tortured by unnumerable unreal and weird claims just as difficult for an Indian to believe. Wovoka promised his people a savior, salvation, and a millennium. So does every Christian sect. Self-abnegation and dancing for its promises are just as believable to the Indian mind as are baptism, counting beads, and confession to the white man.

Most important of all, the Wovokan doctrine came at a time when the Indian was a beaten, frustrated, starved creature, without hope. It came from an Indian, was understandable to an Indian, and answered the deepest longings of his heart. Christianity made the white man no kinder toward the Indian. If anything, it had increased his viciousness, and had made him infinitely less tolerant of native beliefs and ways of life. Wovoka succeeded where Christians had collectively failed, because his doctrine was Indian in origin and Indian in concept, in spite of its vague Christian framework. Unlike the Christians, Wovoka made one great mistake—the setting of a date for his millennium. Had the promise been as ephemeral as that in the New Testament, his religion, in spite of the usual perversions, would have had an enduring quality, and would not have sent the Messiah to his grave in grief and heartbreak.

But the Nevada sun beats down on the untended and forgotten grave of Wovoka, son of Tävibo. It is irony that even its puny marker must remember him as Jack Wilson, pseudo white man, instead of prophet to his own race. He died in sorrow for the three hundred other forgotten dead at Wounded Knee. But fate often has strange manner of weighing out the balances. Wovoka's own grandson, the only son of his daughter Alice, laid down his young life in battle for the life and destiny of the white man's world. Captain Harlan Vidovich, a fighter pilot in Claire Chennault's Flying Tigers, was shot down in action over China in World War II. And the grandfather of Harlan Vidovich was Wovoka, the man who attempted to lift the Indian vision to the skies, but lived only to see it perish in despair.

Perhaps it took another such Indian life to atone for what happened at Wounded Knee.

NOTES

NOTE

1 Mooney's calculations would place his birth at about 1856. See Fourteenth Annual Report of the Bureau of Ethnology, II, p. 771. Wovoka's grave marker states that he died "Sept. 20, 1932, age 74," which would place the date at 1858.

2 *Ibid.*, p. 764.

3 For important material on Wovoka's early life with the Wilson family I am indebted to Mrs. Beth Wilson Ellis, of Yerington, Nevada, daughter of William Wilson.

4 Verification for this "blood mixing" incident was given by Mrs. Beth Wilson Ellis.

5 "The Walker River Paiutes were in the habit, about that time, of making seasonal trips en masse, perched atop the railroad's handy boxcars . . . As hop money could purchase fruit and particularly watermelons, few able bodied Indians passed up the seasonal excursion."—E. A. Dyer, Sr., manuscript, *The Jack Wilson Story*, p. 3.

6 For a study of the Smohalla and Slocum doctrine, see James Mooney, Fourteenth Annual Report of the Bureau of Ethnology, II, pp. 716-731. See also Click Relander, *Drummers and Dreamers, The Story of Smowhala the Prophet*, Caxton, Caldwell, Idaho, 1956.

7 The episode of the ice in the river is still a well-told tale in Mason Valley. Participation of the Wilson brothers in the hoax according to Mrs. Beth Wilson Ellis of Yerington, Nevada.

NOTE

8 As dictated by Edward A. Dyer to E. A. Dyer, Jr., and incorporated in a manuscript *Wizardry, The Jack Wilson Story.* This excerpt is from pages 5 and 6. Used by permission. Edward Dyer, Sr., close confidant of Wovoka, is still living [1957] in Fallon, Nevada.

9 The incident of the salted mine given by Mrs. Beth Wilson Ellis. Method of using the shotgun is told by E. A. Dyer, Sr.

10 There is some opinion that Wovoka was a Mormon Paiute. His only living child, Alice Wilson Vidovich, insists that he never at any time embraced that faith, and no record of such conversion has been found. It is interesting to note, however, that both Wovoka's daughter Alice, and her husband, Andrew Vidovich (half Shoshonean, half Slavonian), are not only converts of the Mormon church, but very staunch members. They live in Schurz, Nevada.

11 Mooney sets date of the eclipse as 1889 (see p. 774). All evidence indicates that Wovoka claimed two definite and great religious experiences, the most profound one, however, being at the time "the sun died." "In our conversation he . . . stated that it was about two years since he had visited heaven and received the great revelation but that it was about four years since he had first taught the dance to his people. The fact that he has different revelations from time to time would account for the discrepancy of statement."—Mooney, p. 772.

12 For the most comprehensive and authentic study of the Wovokan doctrine, its establishment, and spiritual manifestations, see Mooney, pp. 771-791.

13 "He [Wovoka] painted such an enticing picture that a few of his most faithful believers decided to hurry things up by eating wild parsnip root (water hemlock). I personally witnessed the demise of one deluded victim and can attest that it was a long drawn out and agonizing death."—E. A. Dyer, *mss.,* p. 4.

14 Western Indians referred to him as *Numa-Naha,* or "Paiute Father."

15 Mooney, p. 802.

Notes

NOTE

16 Either by treaty arrangement for right-of-way privileges, or by tacit understanding, it was the accepted practice for railroads throughout the west to carry Indian passengers free of charge. Travelers were seldom without the spectacle of blanketed Indians on western trains, although the natives were often forced to take their rides in the baggage cars or atop the engine gondola. Occasionally kind-hearted conductors would allow them sitting-room in the coaches.

17 Pyramid Lake.

18 Porcupine was doubtless in Mormon country.

19 The Shaker influence?

20 For Porcupine's complete statement, see Mooney, pp. 793-796.

21 *Ibid.*, p. 819.

22 Principal, Indian school, Pine Ridge agency.

23 Mooney, p. 797.

24 See *Book of Mormon, passim.*

25 See Bailey, Paul, *Jacob Hamblin, Buckskin Apostle,* Westernlore Press, Los Angeles, 1948

26 Mooney was of the opinion that the Mormons had influential part in the messianic complex among the Paiutes. See Mooney, pp. 792-793.

27 This episode, and the following one dealing with his standing up to a shotgun blast are, in general substance, according to Edward Dyer, Sr., close confidant to the Messiah. *Mss.*, pp. 7, 8, 9. There are many versions of the story, both Indian and white, throughout Mason Valley, but there can be no question that this event, and the belief that Wovoka was impervious to gunshot, had great bearing upon the "bullet-proof" ghost shirts adopted by the Sioux, Arapaho, and Cheyennes.

28 See Johnson, W. Fletcher, *Life of Sitting Bull and History of the Indian War*, p. 206, Edgewood Publishing Co., 1891.

29 Catlin, George, *Manners, Customs, and Condition of the North American Indians*, pp. 208-210, Chatts and Windus, London, 1876.

NOTE

30 Johnson, pp. 39-41.

31 See Vestal, Stanley, *Sitting Bull, Champion of the Sioux.* University of Oklahoma Press, Norman, Okla., 1957.

32 Johnson, pp. 39-41.

33 *Ibid.,* pp. 41-42.

34 *Ibid.,* p 64.

35 *Ibid.,* p. 140.

36 *Ibid.,* pp. 144-147.

37 *Ibid.,* p. 157.

38 *Ibid.,* pp. 157-158.

39 *Ibid.,* pp. 168-169.

40 *Ibid.,* pp. 170-171.

41 See Hyde, George E., *A Sioux Chronicle,* University of Oklahoma Press, Norman, 1956, pp. 285-286. This book gives a detailed and most excellent study of the rise of the ghost dance religion among the Sioux, and the disasters which followed.

42 Johnson, pp. 179-180.

43 Mooney, pp. 877-878.

44 See Johnson, Dorothy M., "Ghost Dance: Last Hope of the Sioux," *Montana, the Magazine of Western History,* summer, 1956. In it is also quoted Senator Carl Mundt's observation on the massacre: "It can hardly be classed as the white man's proudest hour."

45 See Johnson, W. Fletcher, pp. 428-429. See also Hyde, George E., pp. 282-283.

46 Wood, Norman B., *Lives of Famous Indian Chiefs,* L. W. Walter Company, Chicago, pp. 486-487.

47 See Mooney, p. 766.

48 Dyer states that the letters "were almost invariably postmarked Darlington, Oklahoma, and written by one Grant Left-Hand, who appeared to function as a scribe for most of the Indian

Notes

Nation." Grant Left-Hand appears also to have been something of an agent also for Wovoka's holy objects.

49 The Mooney report not only is the best study of Wovoka and his doctrine extant, but traces also the history of other Indian prophets and spiritual leaders throughout the various tribes.

50 Mooney, p. 767.

51 *Ibid.*, p. 767.

52 *Ibid.*, pp. 767-768.

53 *Ibid.*, pp. 768-769.

54 *Ibid.*, pp. 770-771.

55 See Mooney, p. 771.

56 *Ibid.*, p. 50.

57 In the transaction of shirts through Grant Left-Hand and the *doo-mur-eye,* or magic, he performed to prove to his followers that he was inviolate and bullet-proof, Wovoka can scarcely escape blame for the ghost-shirts of the eastern Sioux. He was just as persistent in disclaiming that he had ever posed as the Christ—maintaining that he was a prophet only—though more than one eye-witness account by tribal visitors indicate that he tacitly and willingly allowed the legend to grow, and actually painted or cut scars into his hands and legs as indicative that he had been nailed to the cross. See Porcupine's report, page 111; George Sword's report, page 117.

58 Mooney, pp. 771-773.

59 *Ibid.*, p. 774.

60 Colonel Tim McCoy, himself an authority on the Plains Indian and deeply interested in the Wovokan legend, was of considerable help to the author in piecing out many missing details in the life and experiences of the Paiute Messiah.

A SELECTIVE READING LIST

Book of Mormon, Salt Lake City, various editions.

Burdick, Usher L., *The Last Days of Sitting Bull, Sioux Medicine Chief.* Wirth Bros., Baltimore, Md., 1941.

Mooney, James, *The Ghost Dance Religion and the Sioux Outbreak of 1890,* Part II, Fourteenth Annual Report of the Bureau of Ethnology, House Document No. 230, 54th Congress. Government Printing Office, Washington D. C., 1896.

Morgan, Dale W., *The Humboldt, Highway of the West,* Farrar & Rinehart, New York, 1938.

Humphrey, Seth K., *The Indian Dispossessed,* Boston, Little Brown & Company, 1906.

Johnson, Dorothy M., "Ghost Dance: Last Hope of the Sioux," *Montana, the Magazine of Western History,* Helena, Montana, Summer 1956, pp. 42-50.

Johnson, W. Fletcher, *Life of Sitting Bull and History of the Indian War of 1890-91.* Edgewood Publishing Co., 1891.

Pioneer Nevada, a collection of pioneer incidents. Published by Harold's Club, Reno, Nevada, 1951.

Relander, Click, *Drummers and Dreamers, The Story of Smowhala the Prophet,* Caxton Printers, Caldwell, Idaho, 1956.

Spindler, Will H., *Tragedy Strikes at Wounded Knee,* Gordon Journal Publishing Company, Gordon, Nebraska, 1955.

Standing Bear, Luther, *My People the Sioux,* edited by E. A. Brininstool. Houghton Mifflin Co., Boston, Mass., 1928.

Wellman, Paul J., *Death on Horseback,* J. B. Lippincott Co., Philadelphia, Pa., 1947.

Wood, Norman B., *Lives of Famous Indian Chiefs,* L. W. Walter Co., Chicago, 1906.

INDEX

Index

Index

Wovoka (Jack Wilson) *(Continued)*
revelation and ghost dance, 79-86; second visit to heaven, 86-91; spread of his ghost dance to other tribes, 93-119; efforts to prove himself invulnerable, 121-128; the Plains Tribes pervert the dance with ghost shirts, 154-155; reaction to the public storm over bloodshed in South Dakota, 171; false Messiahs, 171-174; shocked and sorrowed by the Sioux tragedies, 174-176; visited by Arthur Chapman, 175-177; visitors frightened, and in fewer numbers, 178-180; Ed Dyer's assistance in mailing holy objects, 180-182; visited by James Mooney, 182-197; causes of his religion's failure, 199-204; sorrow of his defeat, 204-205; visited by Col. Tim McCoy, 206-207; death and burial, 207-210

Yakima (Indian tribe), 51
Yellow Knife (Sioux), 115, 116
Yellowstone Valley, 140-141
Yerington, Nevada, 14, 103, 188, 201, 206, 208
Y.M.C.A. Hall, Philadelphia, 150
Young, Brigham, 100
Yowaluch, Louis, 51, 54-55

Zhashmocks, the, 29-31